Copyright © 1995 Susan Scheewe Publications
13435 N.E. Whitaker Way, Portland, OR 97230
Phone (503) 254-9100 Fax (503) 252-9508

1

INTRODUCTION TO PAINTING REALISTIC ANIMALS

The secret to painting realistic animals is to take your time and to paint what you see. Study the subject for the color values and the color shapes. Do not be afraid to use strong darks and lights because these are what will give your painting depth. I hope that you will learn some helpful techniques from this book and that you will enjoy your journey through the Bitterroot Backroads where many of these animals live.

ABOUT THE AUTHOR

For as long as I can remember I have been drawing and painting animals. For many years I worked for a large medical corporation and did much of their art work. Having a strong medical background has given me a good understanding of anatomy which helps a great deal when painting any living thing. Later I did portraits for many celebrities and I also did the fine art that was reproduced on about thirty collector plates and figurines. For the past few years I have devoted most of my time to teaching painting and doing workshops. My spare time is spent at home with my family and animals on our small ranch in North Idaho.

For Seminar Information Contact:
Glenice Moore
P.O. Box 224
Hayden Lake, Idaho 83835
(208-683-2150

DEDICATION

This book is dedicated to all of my loyal students, friends and family who were there for me when things were rough and to those who are still there now that things are good and especially to all of the beautiful animals that God gave us to enjoy and to my Alan for his support and patience.

Rights to this book have been reserved. No part of this book is to be reproduced in printed form without written consent of publisher.
Designs may be painted on projects for fun and profit.

PAINT AND MATERIAL LIST

I have listed all of the Paint brands and colors that I have used in this book. I prefer the Shiva Signature Oils because the colors are the closest to natures colors that I have found. I have used this brand for many, many years and have found it to hold up very well. You may use the brands that are available to you or that you are the most comfortable with. You need not rush out to purchase all of the colors that are listed here either. I am sure that you can make do with many of the paints that you have. There are a few colors that I find that I cannot do without and I have put an explanation next to them. If you are not familiar with these colors you may wish to check into them. I am sure that you will enjoy them as much as I do.

OIL PAINT

SHIVA SIGNATURE OILS
Ultra White (warm white)
Brilliant Yellow Light (used for white on animals)
Unbleached Titanium (this is a beautiful cream color)
Ice Blue (light blue gray)
Naples Yellow
Raw Sienna
Burnt Sienna
Raw Umber
Burnt Umber
Van Dyke Brown
Paynes Gray (used to make darks)
Ivory Black
Cobalt Blue
Prussian Blue
Shiva Violet Deep
Manganese Blue
Alizarin Crimson
Cadmium Red
Cadmium Orange
Cadmium Yellow Light
Yellow Citron

WEBER PERMALBA
Misty Gray (used for underpainting)
Paynes Gray (used for dark snow)
Cobalt Violet Hue

GRUMBACHER
Thalo Red Rose
Thalo Blue
English Red (makes a nice pink)
Thalo Yellow Green

ALEXANDER
Deep Orange

ROWNY GEORGIAN
Brown Madder

GRUMBACHER
Zec Gel

MISCELLANEOUS SUPPLIES
Wipe Out Tool
Binney-Smith 55-11 Palette Knife
Jenkins Sta-Brite Varnish
Graphite Paper
Workable Fixative
Lint Free Cloths (Tee Shirt)
Odorless Turpentine

BRUSHES

I have found the brushes that I have listed in this book to work the best for me and the technique that I am trying to teach you in my classes and in this book. They have a nice bounce and hold a good chisel edge and they are not terribly expensive. Some of these brushes are synthetic so they should not be left standing in any cleaning solution. *UNDER NO CIRCUMSTANCE SHOULD YOU APPLY ANY KIND OF LARD OR OIL TO THEM.* Applying any of these things to these brushes will take the bounce out of them and they will be ruined. *YOU MUST HAVE GOOD BRUSHES TO DO A GOOD PAINTING. IF YOUR BRUSHES ARE NOT GOOD YOU WILL FIND YOURSELF STRUGGLING WITH THE TECHNIQUE THAT I WILL BE TRYING TO SHARE WITH YOU AND YOU WILL PROB-ABLY BECOME FRUSTRATED. GOOD BRUSHES AND SMOOTH CANVAS ARE ESSENTIAL IF YOU ARE TO ACHIEVE REALISTIC ANIMALS USING MY METHODS.*

I RECOMMEND:
No. 24 Royal Superb Blend (For all underpainting)
Nos. 2, 4, and 6 Loew Cornell 797-F Series
No. 0 Loew Cornell Mixtique Liner 8050 Series
1 inch and 1/2 inch Langnickle Skywash 1357 Series
1/2 inch Loew Cornell Rake Filbert 7025 Series

CANVAS

Use the smoothest canvas that you can find. Some artists paint on masonite but it requires some preparation so I use my own brand (GLENICE CANVAS) which is a portrait polyester. You will find it very difficult to achieve fine detail on a rough grade canvas as your brushes will skip over the rough surface and the rough canvas will wear your brushes out very quickly. **NEVER USE CANVAS BOARD.** You may obtain information on where to purchase the GLENICE Canvas or any of the other supplies mentioned in this book from the following distributors:

QUALITY ART
106 W. 31st St.
Boise, Id. 83714
(208) 385-0530

SQUARE GRANNY'S
P.O. Box 97
Athol, Id. 83801
(208) 683-2351

BITTERROOT BACKROADS
P.O. Box 224
Hayden Lake, Id. 83835

GENERAL PAINTING TIPS

Doing fur is not difficult if you follow a few basic steps. I cannot stress enough that you either know your subject matter well or that you have good reference material. As well as I know anatomy and animals I still need to use reference material. The following painting tips may help you.

1.   There are three steps to painting fur. If you do not try to skip steps you should not have too much trouble.

   A.   Base in all of the color shapes. Use the middle values for this. Do not try to paint hair at this point. The only place that you will make hair strokes is where the hair touches the background. Where two colors meet, soften the edges with a dry brush or with the Skywash.

   B.   The second step is to paint in clumps of fur. This is to establish hair length and hair direction. Also work in a little more color at this time. I use the 797-F Nos. 2 and 4 for this step.

C.   The third and final step is to detail the fur and intensify the colors and the darks and lights. Use the No. 0 liner to flip in soft, fine hair on the ends of the clumps that you established in Step Two. **SEE COLOR PLATE FOR THE THREE STEPS IN PAINTING FUR.**

2.   There are nine values of every color ranging from dark (almost black) to light (almost white). You must give the illusion that these values exist in your animal paintings. You cannot have just dark and light or your work will look flat and will not have depth.

3.   Use the appropriate highlight colors and do not be afraid to use reflective light. Remember that all light is not white.

4.   Hair grows from the skin out so you should pull your strokes from the skin out. Place the tip of the brush on the canvas and gently press down and as you begin to pull the brush flip the tip of the brush away from the canvas. When using the liner be sure to keep your paint the consistency of ink.

5.   To load the liner, your paint must be like ink. Thin it down by dipping the liner into the clean turpentine and rolling the liner through the paint. Do this each time that you reload the brush. Roll the brush through the paint and pull the brush back at the same time. This will ensure that your brush is well loaded. If the liner is properly loaded you will be able to make many hair strokes. If you get a hair that looks like a pollywog it means that your paint is too thick.

6.   Be very careful not to make your hair strokes look straight and stiff. It should look relaxed and soft. See Fig. 1.

7.   Do not over load your paint brushes. If you are used to painting with heavier paint then perhaps you should get in the habit of wiping your brush on a cloth before putting it to the canvas.

8.   Always use a brush that is compatible in size to the area that you are working on. Using a brush that is too small will give your work a spotty look and if the brush is too large you will not be able to do fine neat work.

9.   I use the Skywash brushes to soften my brush strokes and to even out the paint. They come in several sizes but I use the 1 inch and the 1/2 inch the most. A word of caution: Do not over do when you use these brushes or you will blur or wipe out things that you shouldn't.

10.   It is very important that the hair direction and hair length are correct. When establishing the hair direction think of a clock with the upper most portion being 12 the right middle being 3, the bottom being 6 and the left middle being 9. See Fig. 2.

11.   I brush mix my colors for the following reasons:

    A.   I use very little paint and mixing with a knife will waste paint.

    B.   I like the variance of color that I get by brush mixing and I find it to be much faster than knife mixing.

    C.   If knife mixing is not done correctly it can crush the color pigments in the paint and dull the color.

12.   To keep the paint the correct consistency I always dip the tip of the brush into the small container of clean turpentine that I keep by my palette and then I gently blot it on a lint free cloth before going to the paint.

13.   Use a soft, clean, lint free cloth such as an old tee shirt material. This will work much better than paper towels because it is much more absorbent and it is much easier on your brushes.

14.   I never do the eyes first. I feel that you need to be sure that the head is proportioned correctly. For the order in which to paint your animals see Fig. 3.

15.   I seldom paint in whiskers. If they are not done properly they can ruin an otherwise very nice painting.

16.   After you transfer the pattern onto the canvas you should spray it with Workable Fixative. This will set the lines so that you can paint over them without removing them. Do not, however, overspray or the paint will not want to stick.

17. When your painting is dry to the touch you may want to spray it with a protective finish. I use Jenkins Sta-Brite Varnish. It adds brilliance to the colors and adds depth as well as evening out the finish.

18. I start at the top of the canvas and work down and from the background out. This makes it easier to have more natural looking fur.

19. I do not use mediums and do not recommend them for this technique as they cause the paint to become sticky. I find that just thinning my paint with the turpentine works the best.

20. The best advise that I can give you now is to relax and have fun. Painting realistic animals is a little different than painting landscapes or flowers but once you get these few basic tips down and practice a little you will have a whole new world at your fingertips. I hope that you learn from my book and most of all I hope that you will enjoy doing these lesson plans. These lessons are meant to be used as a guide to learn technique. I hope that you will use what you learn here in your own paintings.

HOW TO START YOUR PAINTING
These steps are recommended for all of the lesson plans in this book.

1. Make a tracing of the pattern that you want to do. Transfer it onto the canvas by placing graphite paper between the traced pattern and the canvas. Draw over the traced pattern with a stylus or pencil. You may want to anchor the pattern with tape to keep it from moving. Before you remove the pattern from the canvas check to be sure that you have transferred all of the pattern. If the traced pattern that you are transferring has dotted lines on it you do not need to transfer them. They are either for reference or they are for you to reapply that portion of the pattern after you have completed part of the painting.

2. Remove the pattern and spray the canvas lightly with the Workable Fixative. Be careful not to over spray.
   *NOTE: If you should lose part of your pattern when you are painting, let the paint dry and then reapply the pattern. Spray lightly with fixative.

3. Read the "General Painting Tips" prior to painting.

4. Read the instructions on the selected lesson plan completely prior to painting. You may want to highlight colors, brushes or special instructions with a highlighter.

5. Arrange your supplies in a manner that is comfortable for you.

6. Have your reference material where you can refer to it often. This is very important. Rather than tearing up your books, I recommend that you make a zerox copy of the instructions so that you can keep it next to you all of the time and you can keep the book open to the reference picture.

7. Even though the technique that you will been learning in this book is wet on wet, don't expect to complete these paintings in one sitting. They have all be designed as one, two or three day workshops. Learn to take your time. Some of the fine detail is best done on dry paint. AGAIN - RELAX AND ENJOY PAINTING REALISTIC ANIMALS.

8. Be sure that you have good light. I use two adjustable lights on my stand-up easel and three on my drafting table. Remember that the light should come from behind you and from the side, never from the front. It is best to paint with natural North light.

" THE SPRING"

CANVAS: 12 x 16 Glenice Canvas or portrait quality canvas

PALETTE

Misty Gray	Ultra White
Brilliant Yellow Light	Unbleached Titanium
Naples Yellow	Raw Sienna
Burnt Sienna	Raw Umber
Burnt Umber	Paynes Gray
Sap Green	Cadmium Yellow Light
Cobalt Blue	Thalo Blue

BRUSHES

No. 24 Royal Superb Blend
Nos. 2, 4, and 6 Loew Cornell 797-F Series
No. 0 Loew Cornell Mixtique Liner 8050 Series
1 Inch and 1/2 Inch Langnickle Skywash 1357 Series

MEDIUM

Odorless Turpentine - You will need one container to clean your brushes in and a small container to keep by your palette to be used to thin your paint.

DIRECTIONS:

1. Read the sections "General Painting Tips" and "How To Start Your Painting".
2. Before you transfer your pattern onto the canvas be sure to read the instructions all the way through.

BACKGROUND

Give the entire canvas a thin even coat of Misty Gray, EXCEPT the deer. Skywash. Use No. 24.

Start in the upper left corner of the canvas with a mixture of Paynes Gray + Sap Green and paint in the area from the upper corner down the left side of the canvas. Refer to the reference picture. You may want to add a small amount of Thalo Blue. The area above the deer's head and shoulder up to the top of the canvas should be painted in with a mixture of Sap Green + Brilliant Yellow Light + Unbleached Titanium and a touch of Thalo Blue. Use an X stroke for the entire background and Skywash to even out the paint.

ROCKS

Paint in the rocks loosely keeping them lighter at the top of the canvas. Use Paynes Gray + Raw Umber and lighten with Misty Gray then Skywash. The rocks at the top of the waterfall are just faint shapes of color. There is not a real definite shape to them. The moss on the rocks is made from the green mix that you used in the background + Cadmium Yellow Light. Add Brilliant Yellow Light to highlight. Use the Nos. 4 and 6 for this.

WATER ON THE WATERFALL

I used the No. 4 and a mixture of Ultra White + Thalo Blue + Sap Green. Keep the color fairly light. Use the chisel edge of the brush and very little paint. Use the 0 liner and Ultra White to highlight the water where it falls over the rocks. Add some dark parts to the water with Thalo Blue + Cobalt Blue and gently Skywash. Add a small line of Paynes Gray where the water touches the rocks. Do not use too much paint. The water should be light and silky. This is a trickling spring not a raging waterfall.

FOLIAGE

Use the Nos. 2 and 4 to paint in the leaf shapes with varying values of the greens that you have already used. Study the Reference Picture. For the pine needles I used the chisel edge of the No. 2. Remember that the light source is coming from above and behind the deer's head. The colors used for the needles and leaves in this area should be very soft. Use some of the light greens that you used in the light area above the deer. The colors may be softened by adding some Misty Gray or Unbleached Titanium. Base in the ground that the deer is standing on with the dark mixture. Push some grass strokes up into the water before the paint dries.

DEER

Paint in the dark areas of the deer with Raw Umber + Paynes Gray. You may wish to add a little Burnt Umber to warm the color up a little. The middle values are Raw Sienna + Burnt Sienna + a little Burnt Umber. The light areas are Raw Sienna + Burnt Sienna + Naples Yellow. The lightest colors are Unbleached Titanium and Brilliant Yellow Light. For the white hair on the under belly and rump use Unbleached Titanium + Raw Umber and a touch of Paynes Gray.

EYES AND NOSE

Use the No. 1 liner and Raw Umber + Paynes Gray to paint in the eyes and the dark on the nose and around the mouth. Highlight with Brilliant Yellow Light.

ANTLERS

Base in with Unbleached Titanium + Raw Umber + Burnt Sienna. Add the darks with Raw Umber + Paynes Gray. Add the highlights with Unbleached Titanium and Brilliant Yellow Light for the tips.

FOREGROUND

Paint in the grass and foliage in the foreground with all of the green mixtures. Add some Cadmium Yellow Light and Brilliant Yellow Light to the greens to make the light grass in front of the deer. Add some final highlights on the foliage near the waterfall. Do not over do this. Just highlight a few leaves.

FINISHING

When the painting is dry it may be sprayed with Jenkins Sta-Brite Varnish. This will provide a protective coating and add brilliance and depth to your colors.

"THE SPRING"
11 x 14

The dotted lines are for reference only and
need not be transferred as the will be painted
over.

"GRAY WOLF"
14 x 18

"GRAY WOLF"

CANVAS: 14 x 18 Glenice Canvas or Portrait Quality Canvas

PALETTE

Misty Gray	Brilliant Yellow Light
Unbleached Titanium	Naples Yellow
Raw Sienna	Ultra White
Burnt Umber	Brown Madder
Paynes Gray	Cobalt Blue
Thalo Red Rose	

BRUSHES

No. 24 Royal Superb Blend
Nos. 2, 4 and 6 Loew Cornell 797-F Series
No. 0 Loew Cornell Mixtique Liner 8050 Series
1 Inch and 1/2 Inch Skywash 1357 Series
1/2 Inch Loew Cornell Rake Filbert 7025 Series

MEDIUMS

Odorless Turpentine - You will need one container to clean your brushes in and a small container to keep by your palette to be used to thin your paint.

DIRECTIONS

1. Read the sections "General Painting Tips" and "How To Start Your Painting".
2. Do not transfer your pattern onto the canvas until you have read the instructions all of the way through.

BACKGROUND

Use the No. 24 Royal and give the entire background a thin even coat of Misty Gray. Skywash to even out the brush strokes and the paint.

Mix Cobalt Blue + Ultra White and use the No. 24 brush to paint in the blue areas of the background. Start at the outside edge of the canvas and use long even strokes towards the center of the canvas. Study the reference picture for the varying values. Try to keep the corners darker than the center. In some areas add more Ultra White so that you will get some nice streaks in the paint. Add some areas of pure Cobalt Blue also. Add some touches of Brown Madder and Thalo Red Rose and then Skywash to soften the color together. *DO NOT LEAVE A HARD EDGE AROUND THE WOLF. FLIP THE BROAD SIDE OF THE BRUSH TOWARDS THE WOLF TO GIVE A SOFT EDGE.* This is very important. If you paint an even edge of background color around the wolf and then let it dry it will be almost impossible to cover later.

WOLF

Put a wash over the wolf with a mixture of Misty Gray + Paynes Gray. Use the No. 24 and again do not paint in hard edges. Flip the brush towards the background color. Use the Nos. 4 and 6 and start adding the darks with a mixture of Paynes Gray + Burnt Umber. Remember that there are three steps to painting fur. Refer to the diagram if necessary. Base in the darks on the ears and down the face. Use a fairly dry brush and do not paint in hard edges. Paint in the light areas with Ultra White + a little Burnt Umber. The neck and the shoulder should be a little darker in value than the light areas on the face. This is *STEP ONE.*

J Lenice ©

WOLF STEP TWO

Now using the Nos. 2, 4, and 6 brushes start with the area between the ears and begin to flip in clumps of fur. Use a dry brush with very little paint to do this. You will establish the hair direction and hair length at this time. Lay the flat tip of the brush to the canvas and gently push down. As you start to pull the brush, lift up and flip the end of the stroke. This would be like a comma or "C" stroke in tole painting. It is important to overlap these strokes. Keep them loose and relaxed. Make them go in different directions. Refer to the reference picture often. Use the Skywash to soften. You may work in more color at this time. Use some Misty Gray + Burnt Umber on the ears and the mask on the face. Add more Misty Gray to this mixture for the area under the eyes and down the center of the nose. Add some touches of Raw Sienna + Unbleached Titanium and Naples Yellow + Unbleached Titanium and soften down with the Skywash. Again use very little paint and a dry brush. Darken the inside of the ears with a mixture of Paynes Gray + Burnt Umber. Lighten the edges by adding Misty Gray. Soften with the Skywash. Now use the No. 2 and 4 and paint in some hair clumps with Misty Gray + Burnt Umber.

Outline the eyes and nose with the Liner brush and a mixture of Paynes Gray + Burnt Umber. Before you fill in the centers of the eyes make sure that you have them set evenly. The left eye will be slightly smaller because the head is turned slightly to the left. Base in the nose with this same dark mixture. Add Misty Gray to contour and highlight with Brilliant Yellow Light. Dry brush a little dark in under the nose and at the mouth line. Use the liner to paint in the mouth line and then soften it out with the No. 2. Add some Ultra White under the eyes and on the muzzle and then soften with the Skywash.

EYES

Base in the eyes with the No. 2 brush and Naples Yellow + a touch of Burnt Umber. Add a little Paynes Gray to this mixture and darken the area under the upper eyelid. Add some pure Naples Yellow in the lower center of the iris. Now paint in the pupil with the No. 2 brush. Use this brush because it keeps the pupil more natural looking. The edges should be soft. Extend the dark color along the under side of the upper eyelid. Add a dot of Cobalt Blue + Misty Gray on the left side of the pupil and highlight the eye with Brilliant Yellow Light.

WOLF STEP THREE

Now go back over the entire wolf and intensify the colors. Darken the darks and brighten the lights. Use the No. 0 Liner to pull in some fine hair but take great caution not to over do this step. Be very careful not to make clumps of fine hair that are joined together at the ends. It will look like the fur has weeds growing out of it. Keep the paint the consistency of ink and keep the strokes loose and relaxed. Use the Skywash to plant the ends of the hair strokes into the fur.

FINISHING

Use the No. 0 Liner to pull tiny hairs down over the eye. Use the Misty Gray + Burnt Umber for this. Watch the hair direction. Use Brilliant Yellow Light to paint in the line around the left side of the muzzle and to make the tiny muzzle hairs. You may want to paint in a few very thin whiskers. Be very careful with this. If you make them too thick or too long or too many it can ruin your painting. When dry spray with Jenkins Sta-Brite Varnish.

"HOWLING GRAY WOLF"

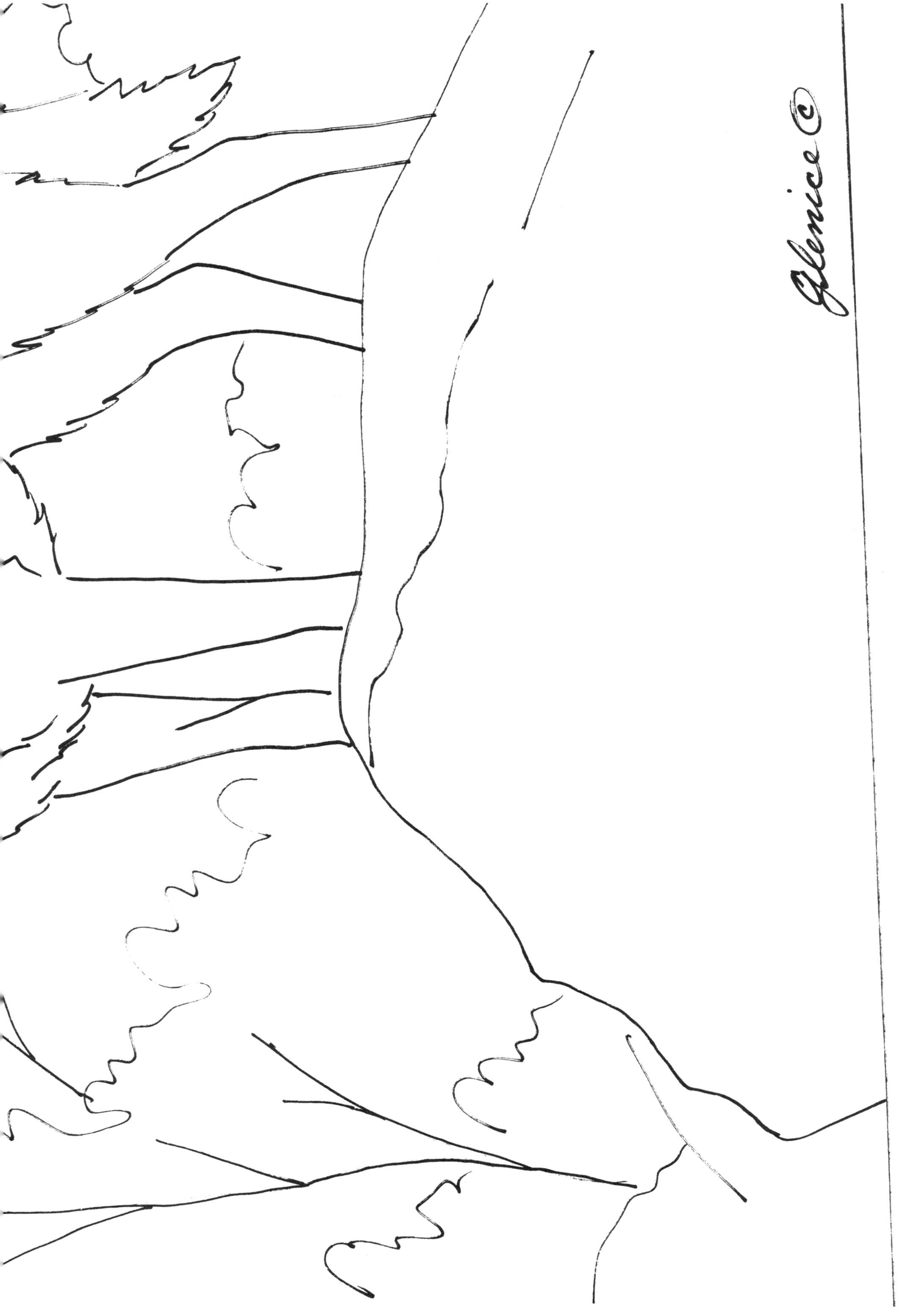
Glenice ©

"HOWLING GRAY WOLF"

CANVAS: 12 x 14 Glenice Canvas or Portrait Quality Canvas

PALETTE

Misty Gray	Ultra White
Brilliant Yellow Light	Unbleached Titanium
Naples Yellow	Raw Sienna
Burnt Sienna	Burnt Umber
Brown Madder	Paynes Gray
Sap Green	Yellow Citron
Cadmium Yellow Light	Deep Orange

BRUSHES

No. 24 Royal Superb Blend
Nos. 2, 4, and 6 Loew Cornell 797-F Series
No. 0 Loew Cornell Mixtique Liner 8050 Series
1 Inch and 1/2 Inch Langnickle Skywash 1357 Series
Binney-Smith 55-11 Palette Knife

MEDIUMS

Zec Gel - Used to texture the rock. It is not necessary for you to use this if you choose not to. The rock may be painted in using the same colors that are listed in the lesson plan. Omit the Zec.

Odorless Turpentine - You will need one container to clean your brushes in and a small container to keep by your palette to be used to thin your paint.

DIRECTIONS

1. Read the instructions all of the way through before you transfer your pattern onto the canvas.
2. Read the sections "General Painting Tips" and "How To Start Your Painting".

BACKGROUND

Give the entire canvas a thin even coat of Misty Gray. Skywash to even out the paint and the brush strokes.

Use the No. 24 Royal for the under painting.

Still using the No. 24 and a mixture of Sap Green + Paynes Gray paint in the upper left corner. Continue down the left side of the canvas. Add some Brown Madder in the bottom left corner. Omit the Paynes Gray and paint in the area just above the rock and in the area above the rock on the right side of the canvas.

Make a mixture of Sap Green + Yellow Citron + Unbleached Titanium and paint in the rest of the background. Refer to the reference picture often for color placement. Add some Brilliant Yellow Light in the upper right corner. Add some touches of Deep Orange and Cadmium Yellow Light along the right side of the canvas. Use the No. 4 797-F and make loose leaf shapes at the edges of the bushes.

LEAVES

Use the Nos. 2 and 4 797-F to paint in the leaf shapes. Use all the colors that you have used in the background. Work light into dark and dark into light. Use the bottom corner of the brush and roll the brush back and forth between your fingers as you tap in the leaf shapes. Be sure to overlap the taps so that the leaves will look like they are connected to a bush and not just hanging in the air. The faster that you move your hand the better your leaves will look. Do not use very much paint on your brush.

BRANCHES AND BACKGROUND ROCKS

Use the No. 0 liner and a mixture of Unbleached Titanium + Burnt Umber to paint in the branches. Use the No. 4 to add some width to the branches once that you have them placed. Add some Paynes Gray to shade and highlight them with Raw Sienna + Naples Yellow. Use Unbleached Titanium for the lightest highlight.

BIG FOREGROUND ROCK

Make a mixture of Misty Gray + Paynes Gray + Burnt Umber and a small amount of Brown Madder. Now add some Zec Gel. Use the palette knife to chop the Zec into the paint. *DO NOT MASH THE PAINT.* Use the edge of the palette knife to almost whip the Zec into the paint. The color that you have mixed will be your middle value on the rock. Pull some of this mixture to the side and add more Misty Gray to lighten. Make a bead of paint along the edge of the palette knife with the middle value and begin laying in the contour of the rock. Make small strokes rather than long ones. Use the flat of the knife on some areas and pat the paint in other areas. Add more Paynes Gray to the middle value to make your dark and lay in some of this. Lay in some of the lightest mixture for the lights. Study the rock formation and pull your knife the way that you want your rock to be contoured. After this layer of paint has dried completely you may add some more color by applying washes. Use Brilliant Yellow Light around the edges of the rock for the back lighting. You may wish to add some touches of Deep Orange, Raw Sienna and maybe some blue made with Paynes Gray + White.

Add some leaves in front of the rock to set it back. Use Sap Green + Paynes Gray for the darks. Add some Cadmium Yellow Light for the light and be sure to watch your light source. Use the same technique that you used for the background leaves.

LIGHT RAYS

Use some thinned down Brilliant Yellow Light and the No. 24 Royal to paint in the light rays. Start at the upper right corner and lightly draw the brush across the canvas. Use very little paint on the canvas and use long even strokes. Gently Skywash.

WOLF

Base in the wolf with a coat of Misty Gray + Burnt Umber. Add the darks with the base coat + Paynes Gray. Add touches of Raw Sienna and Burnt Sienna. Use the chisel edge of the brush to chop in hair clumps. This wolf would be far enough away from you that you would not see fine hair. Use Unbleached Titanium for the light areas and Brilliant Yellow Light for the brightest highlight.

EYE, NOSE AND MOUTH

Use the #0 liner and Burnt Umber + Paynes Gray to paint in the eye, nose and mouth. Highlight the nose with Brilliant Yellow Light and add the teeth with Brilliant Yellow Light.

FINISHING

Add touches of Ultra White to the glow around the edge of the wolf and rock. When the painting is dry you may spray it with Jenkins Sta-Brite Varnish.

"SILVER AND GOLD"

CANVAS: 16 x 20 Glenice Canvas or Portrait Quality Canvas

PALETTE

Misty Gray	Brilliant Yellow Light
Ultra White	Unbleached Titanium
Naples Yellow	Raw Sienna
Burnt Sienna	Raw Umber
Burnt Umber	Paynes Gray
Cobalt Blue	Thalo Blue
Sap Green	

No. 24 Royal Superb Blend
Nos. 2, 4, and 6 Loew Cornell 797-F Series
No. 0 Loew Cornell Mixtique Liner 8050 Series
1 Inch and 1/2 Inch Langnickle Skywash 1357 Series
1/2 Inch Loew Cornell Rake Filbert 7520 Series

MEDIUM

Odorless Turpentine - You will need one container to clean your brushes in and a small container to keep by your palette to be used to thin your paint.

DIRECTIONS

1. Read the sections "General Painting Tips" and "How To Start Your Painting".
2. Before transferring the pattern onto the canvas read the instructions all the way through.

BACKGROUND

Cover the entire canvas *EXCEPT THE UPPER RIGHT CORNER* with a coat of Misty Gray. Leave a fan shaped area bare. Paint this area with Unbleached Titanium. Apply this undercoat with the No. 24 Royal. Skywash.

Starting in the upper right corner with the No. 24 Royal, apply Brilliant Yellow Light. Make a fan shape coming from the corner and flaring out as you work out into the canvas. Next add some Unbleached Titanium + Raw Sienna. Use X strokes and let some of the under painting show through. Next add Raw Sienna + Burnt Sienna. Cover just a little more than half of the canvas working from right to left and work down the canvas just a little more than half way. Paint in the remaining upper portion of the canvas with Paynes Gray + Burnt Umber. Keep the upper left corner dark. Use an X stroke. Skywash. Paint in the snow area at the upper edge of the water with Paynes Gray + Cobalt Blue + a little Thalo Blue and the No. 4 and 6. Paint in the light snow with Misty Gray.

Use Paynes Gray + Burnt Umber to paint in the area behind the pine trees. Skywash.

SNOW

Base in all of the snow with a mixture of Misty Gray + Cobalt Blue and a little Paynes Gray. Skywash.

WATER

Base in the water with Thalo Blue + Misty Gray and a little of the Sap Green and Cobalt Blue. Add a little Paynes Gray at the edge of the bank. Add some Unbleached Titanium in the light part of the water. Mix a little Raw Sienna + Burnt Sienna and with a dry brush paint in a small amount of the gold tones in the water. Make the ripples with Misty Gray. Highlight with Brilliant Yellow Light. Use the No. 2 and 4 brushs for this.

TREES

Use the No. 4 and a rather dry mixture of Misty Gray + Unbleached Titanium to paint in the trees in the background. Keep them subdued in color. Use the chisel edge to paint in the saplings. Keep them loose and relaxed. You may need to add some more of the dark mixture between the trees. Use Burnt Sienna and Raw Sienna to paint in some leaf shapes between the birch trees and the pine trees. Skywash. Add highlights on the larger trees with more Unbleached Titanium, Naples Yellow and Brilliant Yellow Light.

PINE TREES

Use the Rake Filbert and a mixture of Paynes Gray + Sap Green + Burnt Umber to paint in the pine trees. Use the base snow mix to lightly tap in some snow on the boughs. Use Brilliant Yellow Light to flip some grass up over the base of the trees.

BIG BIRCH

Paint in the big birch tree with Misty Gray + Raw Sienna + Burnt Umber. Add some darks with Burnt Umber + Paynes Gray and some lights with Naples Yellow + Unbleached Titanium. Add some small branches. Refer to the reference picture. Mix some Cobalt Blue + Misty Gray to paint in some reflected light on the left side of the tree. Add final highlights with Brilliant Yellow Light.

DEER

Base in the darks on the deer with Burnt Umber + Paynes Gray. Use the Nos. 2 and 4. The middle values are Burnt Sienna + Raw Sienna and the light values are Naples Yellow + Unbleached Titanium. The highlights are Brilliant Yellow Light. Use the No. 0 liner to do the detail on the face. The eyes are Burnt Umber + Paynes Gray with Brilliant Yellow Light for the highlight. Use the same for the nose and the dark markings on the face.

ANTLER

Outline the antlers with the liner and a thin mix of Burnt Umber. Use the No. 2 to base in the middle value with Burnt Umber + Unbleached Titanium. Add the darks with Paynes Gray + Burnt Umber. Use Unbleached Titanium for the lights and Brilliant Yellow Light for the tips.

FINISHING

Add touches of grass in the foreground with Cobalt Blue + Misty Gray and some with Brilliant Yellow Light. Add some gold tones at the base of the big birch tree. Use the liner to paint in a few small branches in the snow and add some frozen weeds with Brilliant Yellow Light.

When the painting is dry it may be sprayed with Jenkins Sta-Brite Varnish to provide a protective coating and to bring out the brilliance and depth of the colors.

"SILVER AND GOLD"

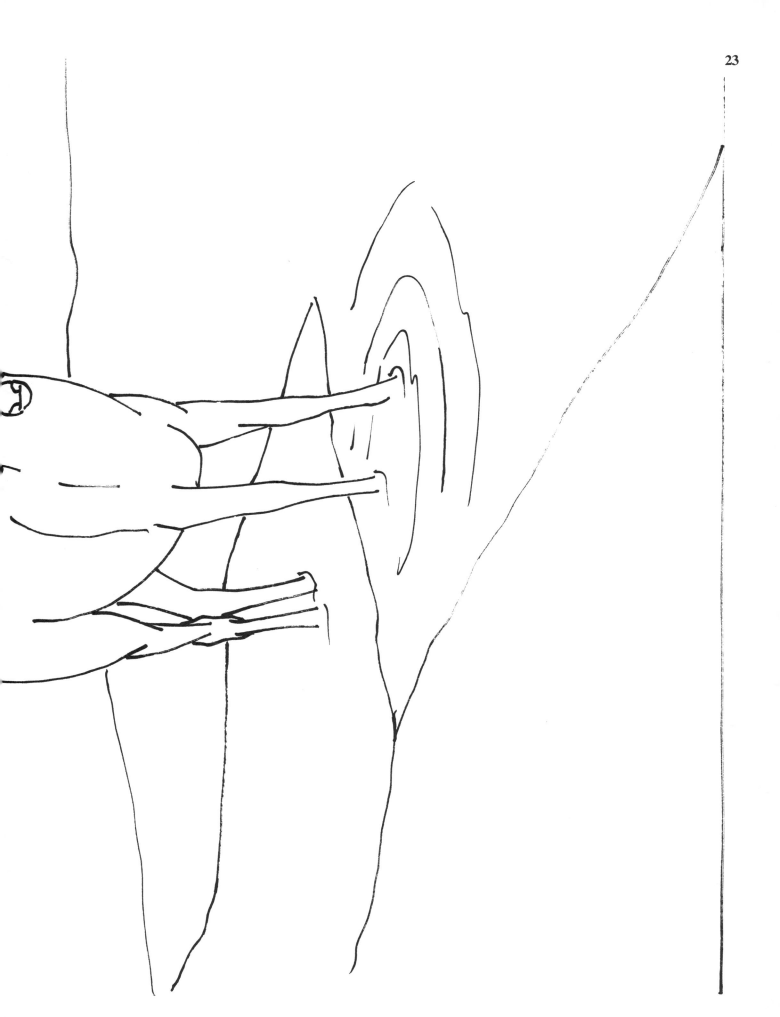

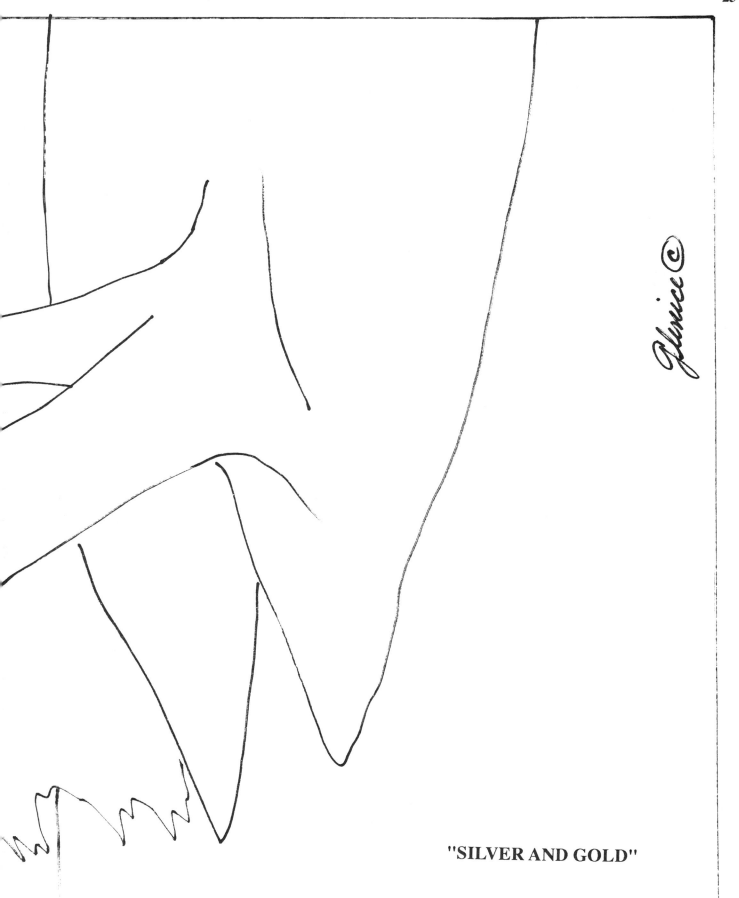

"SILVER AND GOLD"

" THE COUGAR"

CANVAS: 20 x 24 Glenice Canvas or Portrait Quality Canvas.

PALETTE

Misty Gray	Ultra White	
Unbleached Titanium	Naples Yellow	
Raw Sienna	Burnt Sienna	
Raw Umber	Burnt Umber	
Paynes Gray	Ice Blue	
Alizarin Crimson	English Red	
Veridian	Prussian Blue	
Turquoise	Cobalt Blue	
Brilliant Yellow Light		

BRUSHES

No. 24 Royal Superb Blend
Nos. 2, 4, and 6 Loew Cornell 797-F Series
No. 0 Loew Cornell Mixtique Liner 8050 Series
1/2 Inch Loew Cornell Rake Filbert 7520 Series
1 Inch and 1/2 Inch Langnickle Skywash 1357 Series

MEDIUMS

Odorless Turpentine - You will need one container to clean your brushes in and a small container to keep by your palette to be used to thin your paint.

DIRECTIONS

1.   Read the sections "General Painting Tips" and "How To Start Your Painting".
2.   Before you transfer your painting onto the canvas be sure to read the instructions all the way through.

BACKGROUND

Use the No. 24 Royal to apply a thin even coat of Misty Gray over the entire canvas except for the cat and the water. Skywash. Start at the top of the canvas and begin to lay in the snow with a mixture of Ultra White + Cobalt Blue and a touch of Prussian Blue. Do not worry about the pine boughs. We will paint them in later. Add a small amount of Paynes Gray to darken the mixture across the top of the canvas and down the sides. Add Misty Gray and Ultra White for the lighter area in the center of the canvas. Paint in all of the snow. Skywash.

WATER

Base in the water with a mixture of Prussian Blue + Paynes Gray + Veridian. The violet areas are Alizarin Crimson + Prussian Blue + Ice Blue. Lay in the water ripples with the No. 4 chisel edge. Highlight with Misty Gray and with Brilliant Yellow Light.

PINE BOUGHS

You may want to reapply your pattern at this time. Spray very lightly with the fixative. Paint in the snow covered boughs with a mixture of White + Prussian Blue and a little Turquoise Blue. Now use the rake to add some pine needles with Veridian. To darken some of the pine needles add Paynes Gray and to lighten some of them add Misty Gray. Add some dark snow around the pine needles by adding Paynes Gray. Highlight the snow with Ultra White and Brilliant Yellow Light. Add touches of pink with a mixture of Alizarin Crimson + Ultra White.

SILVER AND GOLD
PAGES 20 - 25

THE THREE STEPS IN PAINTING FUR

Fig. 1
Under #6. Correct and incorrect hair strokes.

Fig. 2
Under #10 How to establish hair direction with the clock.

Fig. 3 Under #14 The order in which to paint your animal.

Glenice ©

CAT

These are the colors that are used in the cat:
Base Color: Naples Yellow
Golden Color: Base Color + Raw Sienna
Reddish Color: Golden Color + Burnt Sienna
Darks: Burnt Umber + Raw Umber
Darkest Darks: Add Paynes Gray
Lights: Unbleached Titanium
Lightest Light: Brilliant Yellow Light

Start by basing in the entire cat with the Base Color.
Do not use heavy paint. Skywash.

Now lay in all of the color shapes using the color schedule above. Do not try to do detail hair yet. You are just laying in color shapes.

Use the No. 2 and start on the cat's back and start painting in the hair. Use the chisel edge of the brush and start at the outer edge and work towards the middle and from the top down to the neck. Continue to paint the entire cat in the same manner and in this order: Feet, Legs, Tail, Shoulders, Neck, Ears, Head and Muzzle. Study the reference picture for color patterns. Gently Skywash. Use the 0 liner and paint in some fine detail hair but take care not to overdo this step. Use the small Skywash to paint the hairs into the fur.

EYES

Use the liner and Paynes Gray + Burnt Umber to paint in the eyes. Use Naples Yellow for the light. Pull tiny lashes down from the eyelid.

TONGUE

Use English Red + Misty Gray for the middle value. Add a little more English Red for the pinkish areas. Use Brilliant Yellow Light to highlight. Shape the outside of the tongue with Paynes Gray.

NOSE

Use English Red + Ice Blue. Add Paynes Gray to darken.

WATER

Paint in a tiny line of Paynes Gray under the snow bank. Paint in the reflections of the snow bank with Cobalt Blue + Misty Gray. This should be done with a wash. Paint in the cat's reflection with washes of the colors that you used before. Gently Skywash. The tongue will have the most detail because it is the closest to the cat. Be careful not to over do this step.

DETAILING

Go back over the painting and do your touch up and fine detailing. Add some highlight in the snow with Ultra White and add some pink tones with English Red + Ultra White. This should be done with a wash.

FINISHING

When the painting is dry it can be sprayed with a protective coating of Jenkins Sta-Brite Varnish.

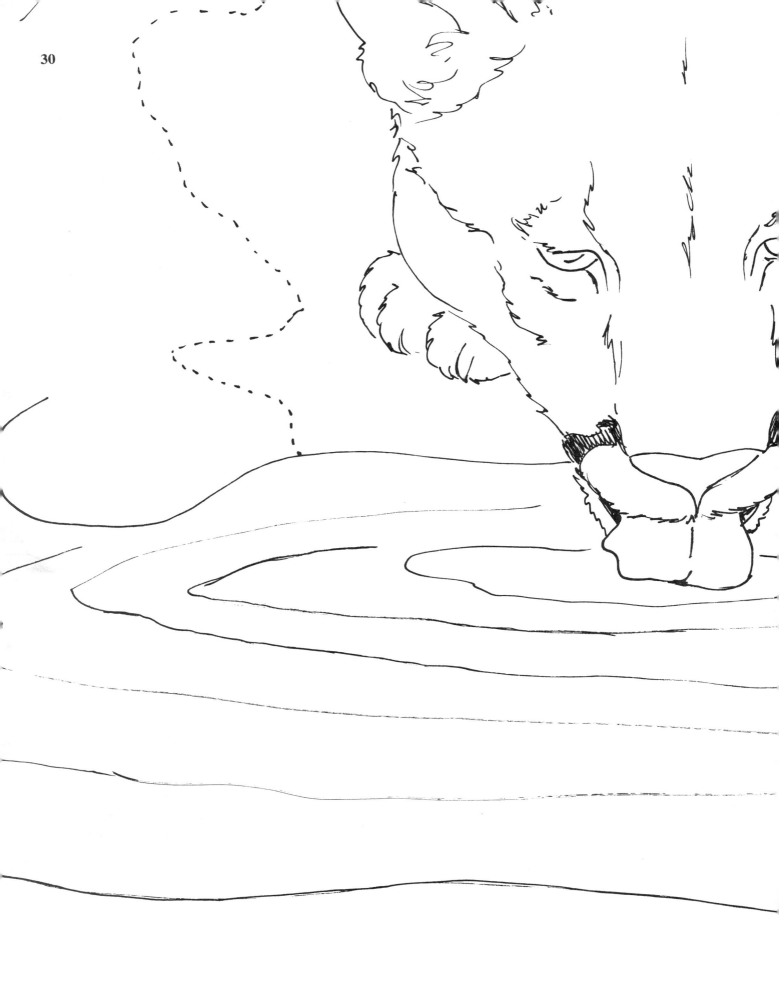

"THE COUGAR"
18 x 24 or 20 x 24

You do not need to transfer the dotted line.
They are for reference only.

Glenice ©

"THE COUGAR"

"RUFFLES"

CANVAS: 16 x 20 Glenice Canvas or Portrait Canvas

PALETTE

Burnt Umber	Burnt Sienna
Raw Sienna	Naples Yellow
Unbleached Titanium	Brilliant Yellow Light
Paynes Gray	Misty Gray
Thalo Blue	Red
Deep Orange	Brown Madder

BRUSHES

No. 24 Royal Superb Blend
Nos. 2, 4 and 6 Loew Cornell 797-F Series
No. 0 Loew Cornell Mixtique Liner 8050 Series
1 Inch and 1/2 Inch Skywash

MEDIUM

Odorless Turpentine - You will need one container to clean your brushes in and a small container to keep by your palette to thin your paint with.

DIRECTIONS

1. Read the sections "General Painting Tips" and "How To Start Your Painting".
2. Read the instructions all of the way through before you start to transfer the pattern onto the canvas.

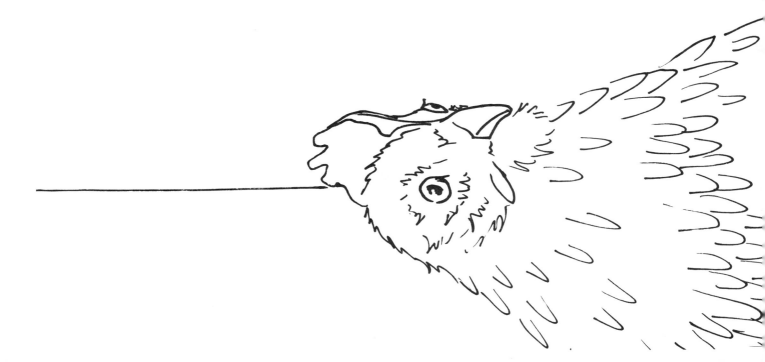

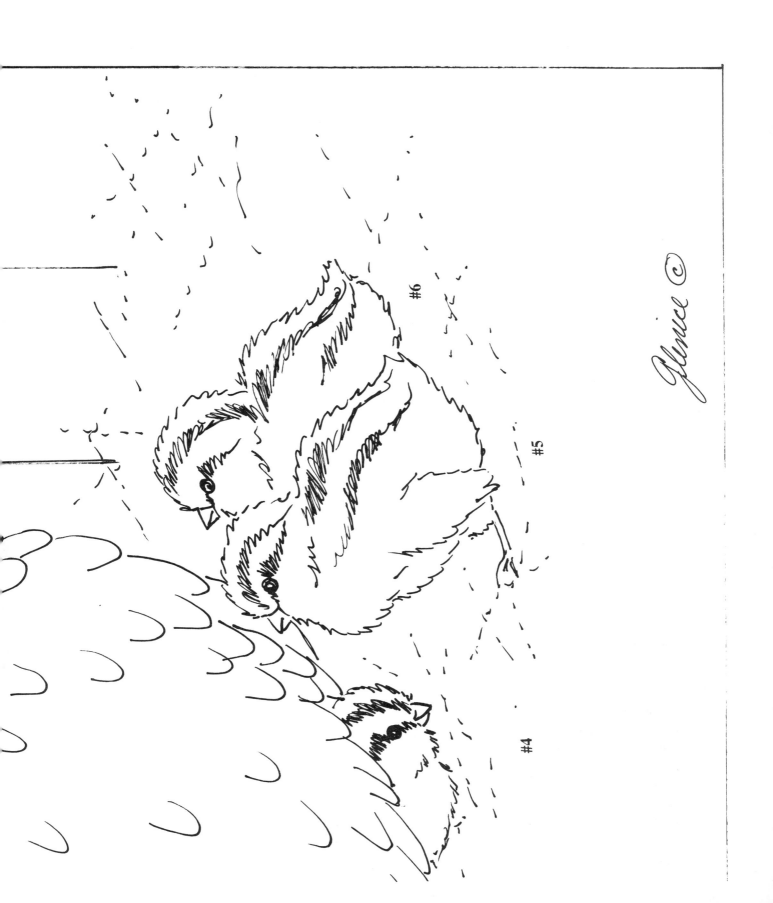

BACKGROUND

Wash in the background with Burnt Umber + Burnt Sienna. Put this wash over the area where the straw will go also. Darken the upper corners by adding Paynes Gray and the bottom corners by adding more Burnt Umber. Skywash. Put this wash in with the No. 24 Royal. Use the chisel edge of the No. 6 and Burnt Umber and paint in the space between the boards. Start at the top of the canvas and pull the brush all the way down the canvas to just below where the straw will start. Skywash to soften. Now use the Nos. 2 and 4 to paint in the knots and lines in the boards. You may need to add some Naples Yellow behind the hen's head and back so that she will stand out more.

Use the No. 4 and some Naples Yellow to paint in some straw shapes next to the wood wall. You do not want this to dry because it will be very hard to cover later.

#3

#2

#1

"RUFFLES"

HEN

Start with the hen's tail. Use the Nos. 4 and 6. Use Paynes Gray + Burnt Umber to base some color in. This should be a wash. Refer to the reference picture often. Use Paynes Gray + Thalo Blue for the dark feathers and highlight with Thalo Blue + Misty Gray. The brown areas are Burnt Umber + Burnt Sienna. Use Naples Yellow + Raw Sienna to highlight. The lighter feathers are Raw Sienna + Burnt Sienna. Highlight these with Raw Sienna + Unbleached Titanium. Continue working in the rest of the feathers on the body. Use Burnt Umber to tip the dark feathers and Burnt Sienna to tip the lighter feathers. On the head and neck use the No. 2. Paint in the comb on the head with Red + a little Burnt Umber. Highlight with Red + Misty Gray.

EYES AND BEAK

Outline the eyes with Burnt Umber + Paynes Gray. Fill in with Burnt Sienna and highlight with Naples Yellow. Darken center with the outline color. Highlight with Brilliant Yellow Light. Outline the beak with Burnt Umber. Fill in with Burnt Umber + Misty Gray. Add nose hole with dark mixture and highlight with Misty Gray.

BABIES NO. TWO, THREE, FIVE AND SIX

Base in the babies with Unbleached Titanium + Burnt Umber. Add more Burnt Umber to darken. Paint in the shaded areas. Add pure Burnt Umber to paint in the stripes. Add touches of Raw Sienna and Burnt Sienna. Highlight with Brilliant Yellow Light.

BABY NO. ONE

Base in the first baby with Unbleached Titanium + Raw Sienna. Add a little Burnt Umber to shade. Use pure Burnt Umber for the stripe. Highlight with Unbleached Titanium.

BABY NO. FOUR

Base in the fourth baby with Unbleached Titanium + Burnt Umber. Add Paynes Gray to shade and highlight with Unbleached Titanium.

EYES AND BEAKS

Use the No. 0 liner and Paynes Gray + Burnt Umber to outline the eyes. Fill in and highlight with Brilliant Yellow Light. Paint in the beaks with Deep Orange and shade with Burnt Umber. Same for the feet and legs.

STRAW

Re-wet the straw with a wash of Burnt Sienna. Use the No. 4 and a mixture of Raw Sienna, Burnt Sienna, Naples Yellow and Unbleached Titanium to paint in the straw. Add some dark straws in the corners with Burnt Umber. Use the chisel edge of the brush and lightly stroke in the straw. Be sure not to make all of the straw stick straight up. It should look like it is laying not growing out of the ground. Make some of the straw bend in the middle like it has been broken.

FINISHING

When the painting is dry it may be sprayed with Jenkins Sta-Brite Varnish to provide a protective finish and to bring out the depth and brilliance of the colors.

"SACRED GROUND"

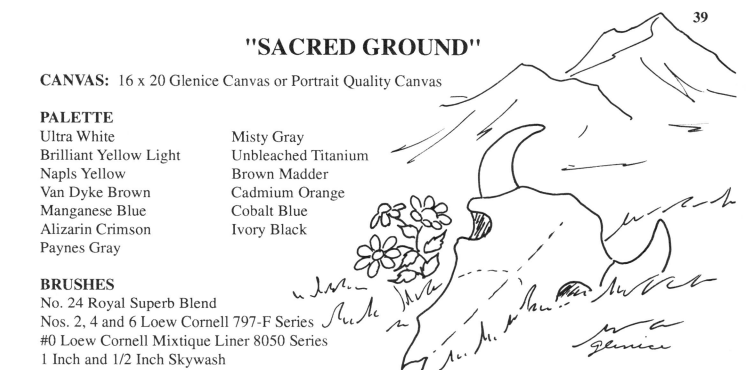

CANVAS: 16 x 20 Glenice Canvas or Portrait Quality Canvas

PALETTE

Ultra White
Brilliant Yellow Light
Napls Yellow
Van Dyke Brown
Manganese Blue
Alizarin Crimson
Paynes Gray

Misty Gray
Unbleached Titanium
Brown Madder
Cadmium Orange
Cobalt Blue
Ivory Black

BRUSHES

No. 24 Royal Superb Blend
Nos. 2, 4 and 6 Loew Cornell 797-F Series
#0 Loew Cornell Mixtique Liner 8050 Series
1 Inch and 1/2 Inch Skywash

MEDIUMS

Odorless Turpentine - You will need one container to clean your brushes in and a small container to keep by your palette to be used to thin your paint.

DIRECTIONS

1.   Read the sections "General Painting Tips" and "How To Start Your Painting".
2.   Do not transfer your pattern onto the canvas until you have read the instructions all of the way through.

BACKGROUND

Cover the entire canvas with a thin even coat of Misty Gray. Skywash. The paint should be thin enough to see your pattern lines.

SKY

Start in the upper right hand corner with a mixture of Paynes Gray + Cobalt Blue. Use the No. 24 Royal. Paint about one third of the way down the canvas adding Misty Gray as you work to the left side of the canvas and as you work down the canvas. Skywash.

CLOUDS

Use the No. 6 and a mix of Misty Gray + Manganese Blue to paint in the clouds. Use the bottom corner of the brush and a very small amount of paint to make little circular motions to push the paint into the background color. Use the Skywash to soften the edges of the clouds. Add some touches of Ultra White + Alizarin Crimson to give a pink glow. Add some Cadmium Orange to this mixture for the golden areas. Use Brilliant Yellow Light around the edges of the clouds where the rays come through the break where the moon will shine through. Soften with the Skywash.

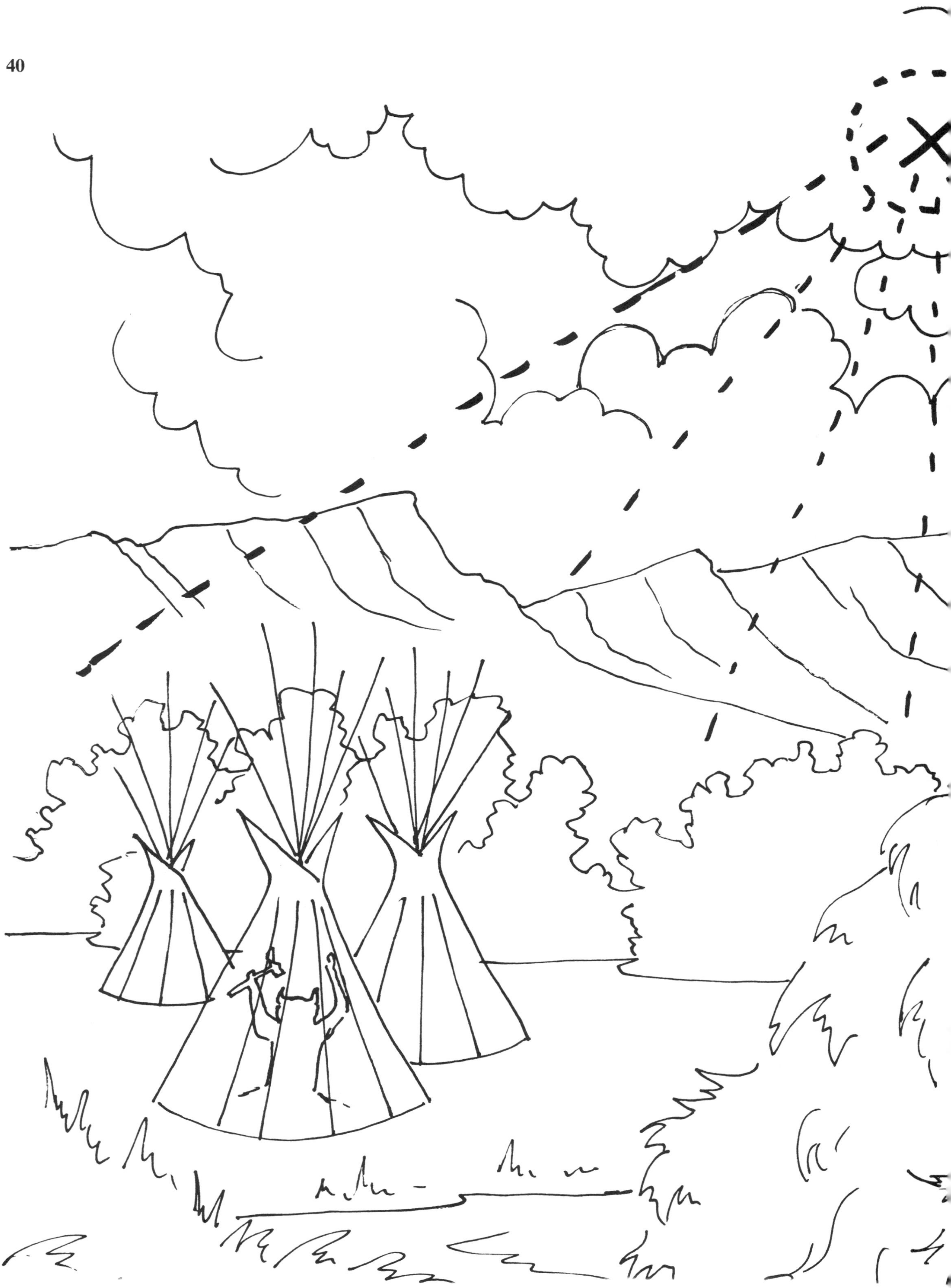

"SACRED GROUND"
16 x 20

Do not trace the dotted lines as they
are for reference only.

"SACRED GROUND"
16 x 20

Do not trace the dotted lines as they
are for reference only.

Glenice ©

43

MOUNTAINS

Use the No 4 and a mix of Cobalt Blue + Paynes Gray + White to paint in the shape of the mountains. This should be a blue gray color. Add more Paynes Gray for the dark areas and add Misty Gray for the light areas. Paint in some pink tones and some gold tones just as you did in the clouds. Remember to study the reference picture. Add Brilliant Yellow Light to add the bright highlights.

TREES

Use the No. 2 and a mix of Paynes Gray + Cobalt Blue. Use the bottom corner of the brush to tap in the color to indicate clumps of leaves. As you lightly tap the brush to the canvas roll it back and forth between your fingers. This will help to prevent your leaves from all going the same direction. Overlap the taps so that the leaves are connected. Use very little paint. Add Misty Gray to lighten. Add some areas of Cobalt Blue + Misty Gray and add a highlight of Cadmium Orange + Alizarin Crimson + Brilliant Yellow Light. Use some of the light blue mix to paint in the ground under the trees.

TEEPEES

Paint in the ground around the teepees with the highlight mixture above and some areas of light, using Unbleached Titanium and Naples Yellow. Paint in some grass using all of the colors that you have used so far.

Make a pinkish gold mixture with Naples Yellow + Brown Madder and base in the teepees. Add some Alizarin Crimson + Naples Yellow at the top and bottom of each teepee. Darken the tops with Burnt Umber + Brown Madder and add some of this color at the bottom also. Use this color to paint in the lodge poles. Where the poles exit the teepees, they should be darkened with Paynes Gray + Burnt Umber. Highlight with Cadmium Orange. Add some light blue mixture to each side of the teepees for reflected light. Use some of the Alizarin Crimson + Naples Yellow to add some glow to the mountains.

LIGHT RAYS

THIS MUST BE DONE ON DRY PAINT. You may either do it now or wait until you have completed the painting and let the paint dry. This must be done quickly and with one sweeping stroke for each light ray. Refer to the pattern for the placement and direction of the rays as they are supposed to be radiating from the moon. Use Brilliant Yellow Light and thin it down with turpentine or you may use a gel or linseed oil. The paint should be thin and transparent but not runny. Use the No. 24 Royal. Hold your brush over the area where the moon would be and then place the brush on the canvas at the opening in the clouds. Quickly pull the brush in an even light stroke. Continue until you have the desired effect. You may want to add touches of the pink and gold tone but again this should be done when the light rays are dry. If you get some of the rays too heavy or thick you may use a brush that has been dampened with turpentine and blotted. Use the same procedure to remove the paint as you used to apply it. Just be careful not to over work the area.

RIVER

Base in the river with Cobalt Blue + Paynes Gray + Misty Gray. Omit the Misty Gray for the darker areas. Paint in the refection with Cadmium Orange + Brown Madder + Alizarin Crimson. Highlight with Brilliant Yellow Light. Use the No. 4 and 6 brushes.

FAR BANK

Base in with Cobalt Blue + Paynes Gray. Use the chisel edge of the brush to flip in some grass strokes. Add Misty Gray to the base mix for the lighter grass and then add some of the pink and gold tones. Darken where the grass touches the water with Paynes Gray.

RUFFLES
PAGES 34 - 38

SACRED GROUND
PAGES 39 - 47

FOREGROUND

Use the No. 24 Royal and a mix of Cobalt Blue+ Paynes Gray to base in the foreground. Keep the lower corners darker, especially the right corner by adding Paynes Gray. Use the chisel edge of the No. 6 to paint in some grass strokes. Mix in some Misty Gray for the light grass and add some pink and gold tones. Use the Nos. 2, 4 and 6 to pull in some finer grass strokes. Keep the strokes loose and flowing. Do not use thick paint as it will not flow. You can also use a dry brush and lift off of the canvas to create grass.

BUFFALO

Put a wash over the entire buffalo with Ultra White + Van Dyke Brown. Paint in the darks by adding Paynes Gray. Use the No. 6 and a mixture of Cobalt Blue + Paynes Gray + Misty Gray to chop in hair clumps. Add more Misty Gray to lighten. Work over the entire buffalo with these mixtures.

After you have painted in all of the hair, start at the outer edge with Brilliant Yellow Light. Use the Nos. 2 and 4 to flip the hair into the background. Work some of this color into some of the hair clumps for highlight. Next to the band of Brilliant Yellow Light, you will now add the pink tones with Alizarin Crimson + Cadmium Orange + Misty Gray. Work the bands of color together but do not blend. Add light into the dark colors and dark into the light colors. Now go back over the entire buffalo and paint in a few fine hairs with the liner brush. Do not over do this step and use the Skywash to plant the ends of the hair into the fur.

NOSE

Use the No. 4 and base in the nose with Van Dyke Brown + Paynes Gray. Contour with Cobalt Blue + Misty Gray. Use Brilliant Yellow Light to highlight.

HORN

Use the No. 4 and base in the horn with Misty Gray. Add Paynes Gray to darken. Pull the paint around the horn to make it look round. Lightly brush in the pink and gold tone and highlight with some Brilliant Yellow Light.

EYE

Use the No. 0 liner and outline the eye with Ivory Black. Use the No. 2 to base in the iris with Burnt Umber + Paynes Gray to create the pupil. Do not paint a round dot. Keep the edges rather vague. Add touches of Misty Gray + Cobalt Blue to contour and highlight with Brilliant Yellow Light. Put a dot of Alizarin Crimson + Cadmium Orange just below the Brilliant Yellow Light.

FINISHING

When your painting is dry you may spray it with Jenkins Sta-Brite Varnish to provide a protective coating and to add brilliance and depth to your colors.

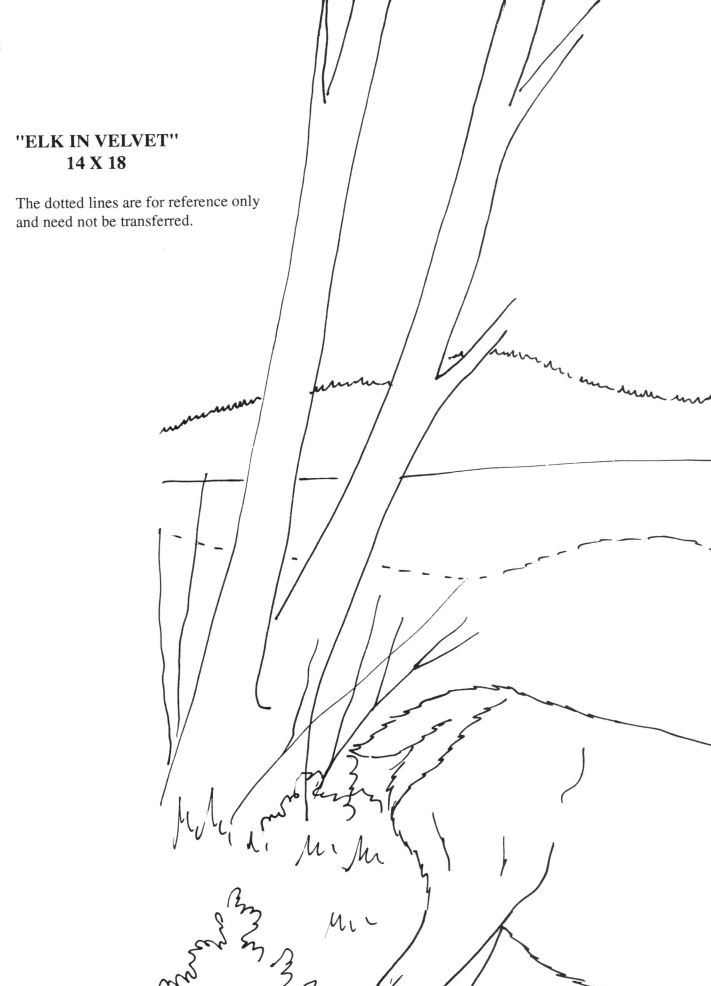

"ELK IN VELVET"
14 X 18

The dotted lines are for reference only
and need not be transferred.

CANVAS: 14 x 18 Glenice Canvas or Portrait Quality Canvas

PALETTE

Misty Gray	Ultra White
Brilliant Yellow Light	Unbleached Titanium
Naples Yellow	Raw Sienna
Burnt Sienna	Burnt Umber
Paynes Gray	Cobalt Blue
Sap Green	Yellow Citron

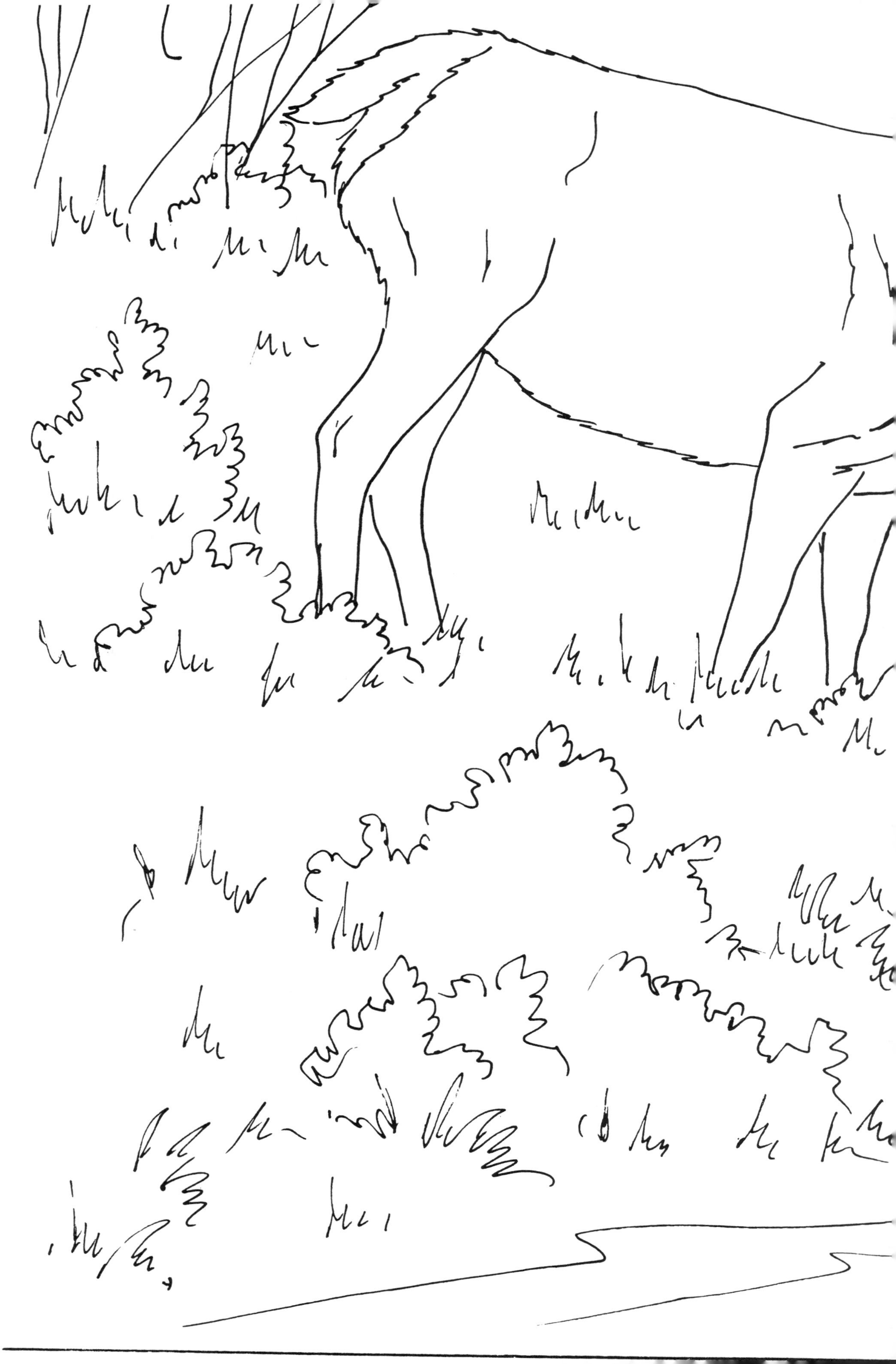

Glenice ©

"ELK IN VELVET"

BRUSHES
No. 24 Royal Superb Blend
Nos. 2, 4, and 6 Loew Cornell 797-F
No. 0 Loew Cornell Mixtique Liner 8050 Series
1 Inch and 1/2 Inch Langnickle Skywash 1357 Series
1/2 Inch Loew Cornell Rake Filbert 7025 Series

MEDIUMS
Odorless Turpentine - You will need one container to clean your brushes in and a small container to keep by your palette to be used to thin your paint.

DIRECTIONS
1.　　Read the sections "General Painting Tips" and "How To Start Your Painting".
2.　　Read the instructions all of the way through before you transfer your pattern onto the canvas.

BACKGROUND
Cover the sky, mountain and water area with a thin even coat of Misty Gray. Skywash to even out the paint.

SKY AND LAKE
Make a mixture of Cobalt Blue + Ultra White and use the No. 24 to paint in the sky. Keep the color a little darker at the top of the canvas. Lighten the color with more Ultra White as you paint down to the water. Paint over the area where the mountains will be. Use the lightest sky color + Ultra White to paint in the clouds. Use the bottom edge of the No. 6 and make small circular motions pushing the paint into the background color. Fill in the rest of the cloud body with the same color and Skywash to soften.

Paint in the lake with the same colors that you used in the sky. Reverse the values keeping the color lighter near the area where the mountains will be and intensifying the color as you work to the bottom of the canvas. Pull the brush strokes back and forth across the canvas. Skywash to even out the paint.

MOUNTAINS
Mix some of the sky color with Sap Green + Paynes Gray to paint in the mountain shapes. Use the Nos. 6 and 4. Wiggle the chisel edge of the brush along the top of the mountains to make the tree line. Add dark areas with base color + Paynes Gray. The lighter areas are the base color + Yellow Citron. Refer to the reference picture often. Use the dark value to paint in the reflection. Skywash the reflection. Add a little Ultra White along the shore.

Paint in the small mountain in the front with deeper values of the colors you used in the back mountains. Paint in the reflection and Skywash. Add Ultra White along the shore.

Use the No. 4 and Ultra White to paint in the ripple lines in the water. Do not paint the water in the bottom right corner yet. You should just have a blue wash on this area now.

BIRCH TREES
Use the No. 4 and a mixture of Misty Gray + Burnt Umber to base in the trees. Add the darks with Burnt Umber + Paynes Gray. Pull the brush around the tree. Lay the chisel edge vertically and flip it towards the center of the tree. Paint in the light areas the same way on the other side of the trees using Brilliant Yellow Light. Paint in some branches. Do not paint in the leaves at this time.

FOREGROUND

Use the rake filbert and a mixture of Paynes Gray + Sap Green + Misty Gray and tap in some tiny leaf shapes for the bushes along the water. This color should be the middle value of the bushes. Darken with more Paynes Gray and lighten with Brilliant Yellow Light. Refer to the reference picture.

Base in the ground with a wash of Burnt Sienna + Raw Sienna + Unbleached Titanium. Work in some darker values near the bank by the water. Add some touches of Naples Yellow + Unbleached Titanium for the lighter areas.

Use the rake filbert and a mixture of Sap Green + Yellow Citron to base in the grass. Add the darker grass with Sap Green + Paynes Gray. Do not make this color too dark. Add lighter values with Yellow Citron and Unbleached Titanium. Add the remaining bushes with the same colors and technique that you used in the bushes along the bank.

ELK

Use the Nos. 2, 4, and 6 brushes. Start with Misty Gray + Burnt Umber and paint in the dark areas. Add Paynes Gray to this mix and paint in the legs on the far side of the elk. Paint in the base color on the body with Unbleached Titanium + Burnt Sienna + Raw Sienna + a touch of Burnt Umber. Darken this value and paint in the muscles. Soften with the Skywash. Paint in the rump with Unbleached Titanium + a touch each of Raw Sienna and Burnt Sienna. Highlight the rump with Brilliant Yellow Light. Highlight the body with Raw Sienna + Naples Yellow + Unbleached Titanium. Add Burnt Umber + Paynes Gray to deepen the darks on the ears, face and neck. Outline the nose and eyes with the liner and the dark mixture. Fill in and highlight with Brilliant Yellow Light.

ANTLERS

Use the No. 2 and a mixture of Unbleached Titanium + Raw Sienna + Burnt Umber to base in the antlers. Remember that this elk is in the velvet stage and the antlers will have round ends on them rather than pointed. Add the darks with base mixture + Burnt Umber and the lights are Unbleached Titanium and Brilliant Yellow Light for the tips.

TREE LEAVES

Use and Nos. 2 and 4 and the greens that you used in the grass. Base in the leaf masses letting some of the sky show through. Tap in some small leaf shapes. Remember to work from dark to light.

WATER IN FOREGROUND

Re-wet the water in the lower corner with a wash of Cobalt Blue. Mix some Sap Green + Ultra White + Cobalt Blue and paint in ripples. Keep adding white as you work towards the shore. Let some of the brown area show to make it look like the water is washing up on the shore.

FINISHING

When the painting is dry it should be sprayed with a protective coating of Jenkins Sta-Brite Varnish. This will also add depth and brilliance to your colors.

"THE GRIZZLY BEAR"

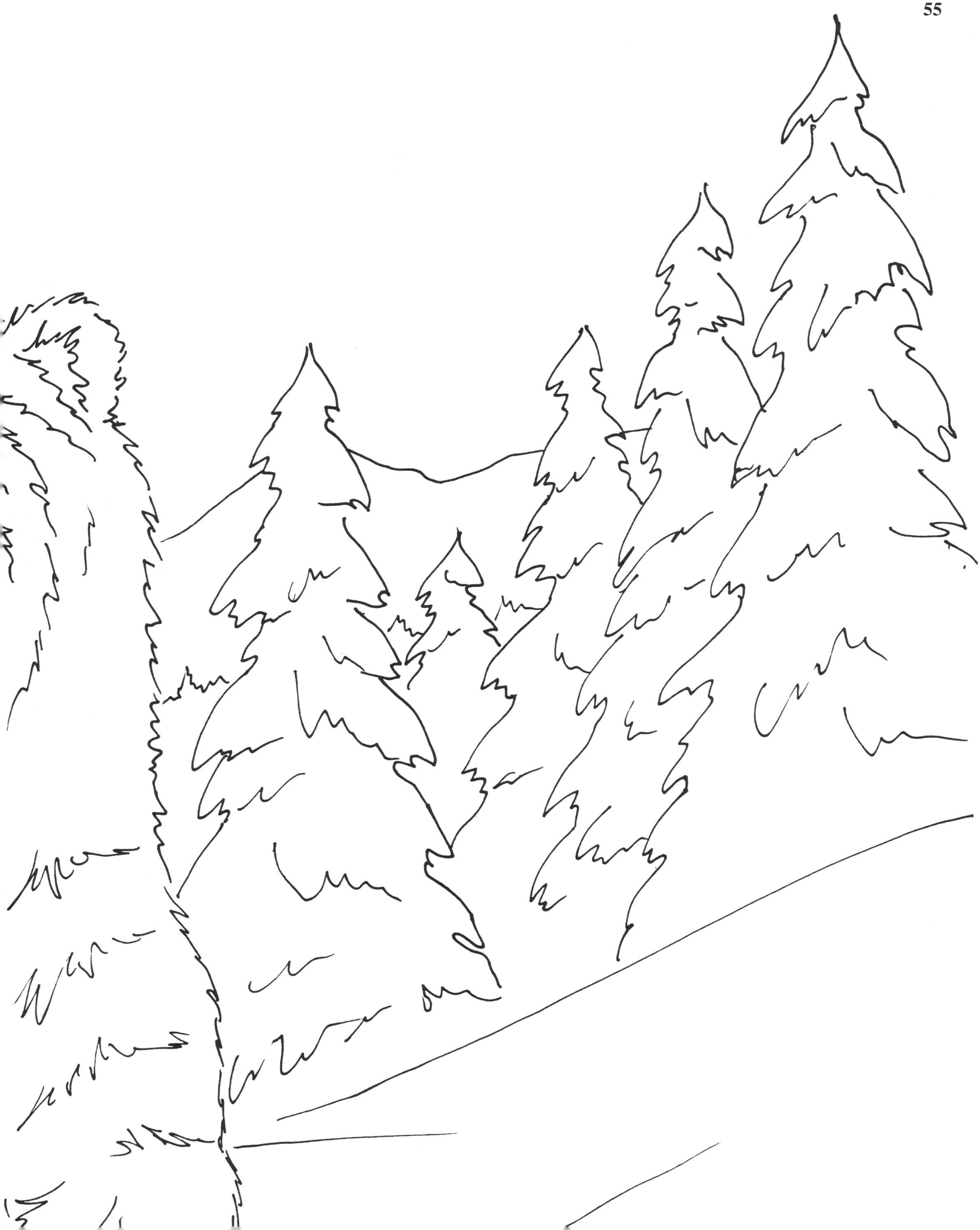

Glenice ©

"THE GRIZZLY BEAR"

CANVAS: 16 x 20 Glenice Canvas or Portrait Quality Canvas

PALETTE

Unbleached Titanium	Brilliant Yellow Light
Ultra White	Misty Gray
Naples Yellow	Raw Sienna
Burnt Sienna	Burnt Umber
Paynes Gray-Shiva	Ivory Black
Turquoise	Thalo Blue
Veridian	English Red
Paynes Gray-Permalba	

NOTE: I have asked for two different brands of Paynes Gray because I use the Permalba brand for the snow and the Shiva brand for the fur because it is blacker.

BRUSHES

No. 24 Royal Superb Blend
Nos. 2, 4 and 6 Loew Cornell 797-F Series
No. 0 Loew Cornell Mixtique Liner 8050 Series
1 Inch and 1/2 Inch Skywash 1357 Series
1/2 Inch Loew Cornell Rake Filbert 7025 Series

MEDIUMS

Odorless Turpentine - You will need one container to clean your brushes in and a small container to keep by your palette to be used to thin your paint.

Jenkins Sta-Brite Varnish for your completed painting.

DIRECTIONS

1. Read the sections "General Painting Tips" and "How To Start Your Painting".
2. Do not transfer your pattern onto the canvas until you have read the instructions all of the way through.

BACKGROUND

Give the entire canvas a thin even coat of Misty Gray. Use the No. 24 Royal Superb Blend for this. Skywash. This coat of paint should be thin enough to see your transferred pattern through.

SKY

Use the No. 24 Royal Superb Blend and a mixture of Misty Gray + Thalo Blue + Turquoise and start at the top of the canvas. Work across and about 1/3rd of the way down your canvas lightening your color by adding more Misty Gray each time that you reload your brush. Soften with the Skywash.

CLOUDS

Use some of the lightest sky color and add some Ultra White to lay in the clouds. Keep them light and wispy. Use the bottom corner of the No. 4 and a small amount of paint. Make small circular strokes pushing the paint into the sky color. Use the Skywash brushes to soften the edges. Gently brush the paint back into the body of the cloud. Add a small amount of English Red to your cloud mix and add some blush to your clouds. Soften with the Skywash. Use Brilliant Yellow Light to highlight the edges of the clouds and again use the Skywash to soften the edges.

SHORTY
PAGES 62 -66

MOUNTAINS

Mix Thalo Blue + English Red + Misty Gray to form a violet gray color. This will be the middle value for the mountains. Use the chisel edge of the No. 6 to paint in the ridge of the peaks. Lay the brush flat on the canvas (vertically) and drag the brush across the canvas moving it up and down at the same time to create the ridge. Be sure not to make all of the peaks the same size. Brush the color down towards the tree line. Do not add much more paint because you want to create a misty look at the base of the mountains. Skywash. Darken this color by adding some Permalba Paynes Gray and a little more Thalo Blue and paint in the shadow areas. Be sure to pay attention to the light source. Lay in the highlights with Brilliant Yellow Light + English Red. Soften with the Skywash.

TREE COVERED MOUNTAINS

Use a mixture of Thalo Blue + Veridian to lay in the tree covered mountain at the base of the first mountain. Use the No. 4. Load the brush on one side only and lay it on its side at a vertical angle and wiggle it up and down as you move it from left to right. This will establish your tree line. After doing this, paint in the rest of this area. Add some lighter color by adding some Misty Gray. Use the same stoke to indicate the tops of some trees. Highlight with Brilliant Yellow Light. Gently Skywash to soften the strokes.

TREES

Use a darker value of the Veridian + Thalo Blue to lay in the larger trees. You may want to add some Permalba Paynes Gray. *DO NOT APPLY THIS PAINT HEAVILY.* Use the 1/2 inch Rake Filbert. *BE VERY CAREFUL NOT TO OVER LOAD THIS BRUSH.* Use a fairly dry mixture of paint and a very light bouncy stroke. Place the tip of the brush vertically on the canvas and lightly press down and sideways letting the brush spring up and away from the canvas. Keep one side of the tree darker than the other. Put snow on the top of the branches with Brilliant Yellow Light. You should pick up some of the blue color when you do this wet on wet. That will give your snow a bluish cast. After the paint dries you may want to add some touches of Ultra White to highlight the highlight.

SNOW

Base in the snow with the No. 24 and a mixture of Ultra White + Thalo Blue + Turquoise. After applying a thin even coat of this mixture to the snow use the Skywash to even out the paint. Add more Ultra White for the highlights and more blue for the shadows. Work the snow up into the base of the big trees on the right and add some Permalba Paynes Gray for shading. Be sure to use long even flowing strokes. Apply enough pressure to the brush to assure even distribution of the paint. Skywash.

BEAR

Use the No. 2 and Unbleached Titanium to paint in the outside edge of the bear on the left. Overlap your strokes to give the hair a soft look. Paint in the outside edge of the ears, neck, back and hind leg. This is the side that your light source is hitting so these will be your strongest highlights. *Do not try to do detail at this stage. THIS IS STEP ONE. Where two colors come together and at the outside edge of the fur, you will make fur clumps.* This is done by using the No. 2 or 4 and using a "C" or comma stroke.

Next paint in the yellow tones with Unbleached Titanium + Naples Yellow. The next color is made by adding Raw Sienna. *REFER CONSTANTLY TO YOUR REFERENCE PICTURE.* Keep working from the outside to the center of the body. Notice that each band of color gets darker.

Now make a mixture of Raw Sienna + Burnt Sienna and work in the next color. Next drop the Raw Sienna and add Burnt Umber. Next drop Burnt Sienna, add Paynes Gray (Shiva). Use this for all of the darkest parts.

"SHORTY"
14 x 18

The dotted lines need not be transferred.
They are for reference only.

Glenice ©

"SHORTY"

CANVAS: 14 x 18 Glenice Canvas or Portrait Quality Canvas

PALETTE

Brilliant Yellow Light   Unbleached Titanium
Ice Blue   Naples Yellow
Burnt Umber   Paynes Gray
Ivory Black   Raw Umber
Yellow Citron   Sap Green
Turquoise   Cobalt Violet Hue
Burnt Sienna

BRUSHES

No. 24 Royal Superb Blend
Nos. 2, 4 and 6 Loew Cornell 797-F Series
No. 0 Loew Cornell Mixtique Liner 8050 Series
1 Inch and 1/2 Inch Skywash 1357 Series
1/2 Inch Loew Cornell Rake Filbert 7025 Series

MEDIUMS

Odorless Turpentine - You will need one container to clean your brushes in and a small container to keep by your palette to be used to thin your paint.

DIRECTIONS

1. Read the sections "General Painting Tips" and "How To Start Your Painting".
2. Do not transfer your pattern onto the canvas until you have read the instructions all of the way through.
3. Study the reference picture.

BACKGROUND

Use the No. 24 Royal Superb Blend and a mixture of Sap Green + Paynes Gray and a touch of Turquoise to paint in the upper corners of the canvas. Work this color across the top and down the sides. Use a criss-cross stroke. As you work towards the center of the canvas omit the Paynes Gray and add more Turquoise and Ice Blue. Add Brilliant Yellow Light to make the glow around the bear's head. The entire canvas should be covered except the bear. Use the Skywash to even out the paint.

BUSHES

Block in the bushes behind the chest and back with Sap Green + Turquoise. Highlight with Yellow Citron. Use the Nos. 4 and 6 brushes to block in the leafy shapes lightly.

Paint in the bushes in the bottom corners of the canvas with Sap Green + Paynes Gray and a little Turquoise. This mixture should be a dark green color. Make leaf shapes at the edges of the bushes. Highlight with Sap Green + Ice Blue and Sap Green + Brilliant Yellow Light. Paint in the light rays with the highlight color. Thin the paint down so that it is transparent. Do not make the paint runny. The under paint must be dry before you do this step. Use the No. 24 Royal. Make long even strokes with very little paint on the brush.

PINE BOUGHS

Use the Rake Filbert and Sap Green + Turquoise + Paynes Gray to tap in the pine boughs. Do not overload this brush with paint. Use the tip to bounce in the tiny pine needles. Practice on a piece of palette paper. Lightly Skywash to set the branches back.

CLEARING AND PATH

Use the No. 6 797-F and a mixture of Yellow Citron + Ice Blue + a little Turquoise to paint in the path and clearing. Highlight with Yellow Citron + Ice Blue. Use the Rake Filbert to add some grass in the clearing and along the path. Watch the size of the grass. Soften with the Skywash.

BEAR

Use the No. 2 797-F and Ivory Black to paint in the darkest parts of the bear. Study the reference picture. Make the body hair stick out into the background rather than painting a smooth edge. Be sure to watch the hair direction and the hair length. Mix the middle values with Paynes Gray + Ice Blue + Ivory Black and paint in all of the middle values on the bear. Paint in the tan markings on the bears face with Unbleached Titanium + Raw Umber and a touch of Burnt Sienna. Shade with more Raw Umber. Highlight the bears head, ears and shoulders with Cobalt Violet Hue + Ice Blue. Add some of this color mixture on the bears side and arms and then add some Turquoise + Brilliant Yellow Light. Use the No. 0 Liner to flip in a few fine hairs.

The light hair on the bear's chest is Brilliant Yellow Light.

CLAWS

The claws are Burnt Sienna + Unbleached Titanium. Highlight with Unbleached Titanium. You may want to add a little Paynes Gray to shade them.

EYES

Use the No. 0 Liner to draw in the outlines of the eyes with thinned down Ivory Black. Fill in and highlight with Brilliant Yellow Light.

NOSE

Base in the nose with Ice Blue + Paynes Gray. Contour with Ivory Black and highlight with Brilliant Yellow Light.

LEAVES

Paint in the leaves that are in front of the bear's leg with the Nos. 2 and 4 and the green mixture that you used on the rest of the bush. Highlight with Cobalt Violet Hue, Yellow Citron and Turquoise.

FINISHING

When the painting is dry it may be sprayed with Jenkins Sta-Brite Varnish.

BEAR STEP TWO

This is where we will establish hair direction and hair length. I call this clumping. Be very careful not to apply the paint too heavy or you will not be able to achieve fine detail.

Use the Nos. 2 and 4 for this step. Start at the legs and work up to the ruff around the face and then stop. Work from the bottom up and the outside in to the middle because this is the way that the hair lays. Now do the ears, top of the head and work down the face doing the muzzle last. Use the same colors but intensify them. Gently Skywash. DO NOT PRESS TOO HARD OR OVER DO THIS STEP.

EYES AND NOSE

Use the liner and Black + Burnt Umber to outline the nose and eyes. Fill the nose in with this color. Shape the nose with Misty Gray and highlight with Brilliant Yellow Light.

Fill the eyes in with Burnt Sienna and add Raw Sienna for the light parts. Highlight with Brilliant Yellow Light.

FINISHING

Use the #0 Liner to pull a few fine hairs on the bear's body. Keep the paint the consistency of ink. If the paint is too thick, you will get an uneven look to the strokes and if the paint is too thin the hairs will be too thick or too bright or too faint. Do not over do this step and remember that the hair grows from the skin out so the hair should be painted that way.

Also keep in mind the hair length. The hair on the head is much shorter than the hair on the body.

Use this step to add brilliant highlights with Brilliant Yellow Light and darks with Burnt Umber + Black.

When the painting is dry it should be sprayed with a protective coating of Jenkins Sta-Brite Varnish. This will bring out your colors and add depth to your paintings.

"DUSTY THE PAINT COLT'"

MEDIUM

Odorless Turpentine - You will need one container to lean your brushes in and a small container to keep by your palette to be used to thin your paint.

DIRECTIONS

1. Read the sections "General Painting Tips" and "How To Start Your Painting".
2. Before you transfer your pattern onto the canvas be sure to read he instructions all the way through.

BACKGROUND

Use the No. 24 Royal and a mixture of Shiva Violet Deep and Paynes Gray to paint in the upper corners of the canvas. Add Ice Blue to this mix and paint in the dark areas at the top of the canvas. Add some Burnt Umber and Misty Gray and start working down. Paint in the areas that indicate dirt and leave blank areas where the grass will go. Paint in the grass with variations of mixtures made with Sap Green, Veridian, Yellow Citron and Unbleached Titanium. Use the Brilliant Yellow for highlight. *REFER TO THE REFERENCE PICTURE CONSTANTLY.*

The shadows that are cast by the brush may be painted in with Cobalt Blue + Violet + Paynes Gray. Keep the values soft and soften with the Skywash.

Continue to work down the canvas. Lay in all of the color shapes. The light area behind the colt's legs is Unbleached Titanium. Use Cobalt Blue + Violet + Misty Gray for the shadow area. Also, use this color as the middle value in the rocks. Shade on the rocks is this color + Burnt Umber and Paynes Gray. Highlight them with Misty Gray and Unbleached Titanium.

COLT

Start with the ears. Use the No. 2 to base in the darkest part of the ear with Van Dyke Brown. Add some Paynes Gray if this is not dark enough.

The colors that you will be using for the colt are as follows:

DARK BROWN: Burnt Sienna + Raw Umber. You may need to add a little Burnt Umber to soften the tone.

LIGHT BROWN: Burnt Sienna + Naples Yellow

HIGHLIGHT ON BROWNS: Unbleached Titanium + Brilliant Yellow Light.

DARK WHITES: Ultra White + Van Dyke Brown OR Paynes Gray

MIDDLE WHITES: Ultra White + smaller amount of Van Dyke Brown or Paynes Gray

LIGHT WHITES: Ultra White and/or Brilliant Yellow Light

Base in all of the colors on your colt. Use the Nos. 2, 4, and 6 brushes. DO NOT DO THE MANE AND TAIL YET.

DETAILING

Start at the top of the canvas and work in more color and fine grass strokes. Move down the canvas intensifying your colors. Use the Skywash to soften.

COLT

Again start at the ears and work down the face. The pink on the muzzle is Misty Gray + Burnt Sienna. Outline the eye with Paynes Gray + Burnt Umber. The iris is Cobalt Blue + Misty Gray. Darken the center with Paynes Gray and highlight with Brilliant Yellow Light. Darken the inside of the nostril with Burnt Umber + Paynes Gray.

Once you have completed detailing the colt's body you may add the mane and tail. Start with the dark brown and work out to the lightest brown mix. The hooves are Misty Gray + Burnt Umber. Highlight with Unbleached Titanium and shade with Paynes Gray.

Once the painting is dry you may spray it with Jenkins Sta-Brite Varnish. This will not only provide a protective coating but will add brilliance to your colors and depth to your painting.

"DUSTY THE PAINT COLT"

CANVAS: 14 x 18 Glenice Canvas or Portrait Quality Canvas

PALETTE

Misty Gray	Ultra White
Brilliant Yellow Light	Unbleached Titanium
Naples Yellow	Raw Sienna
Burnt Sienna	Burnt Umber
Van Dyke Brown	Paynes Gray
Ivory Black	Cobalt Blue
Shiva Violet Deep	Sap Green
Yellow Citron	Ice Blue

BRUSHES

No. 24 Royal Superb Blend
Nos. 2, 4, and 6 Loew Cornell 797-F
No. 0 Loew Cornell Mixtique Liner 8050
1/2 Inch Loew Cornell Rake Filbert 7025
1 Inch and 1/2 Inch Langnickle Skywash 1357

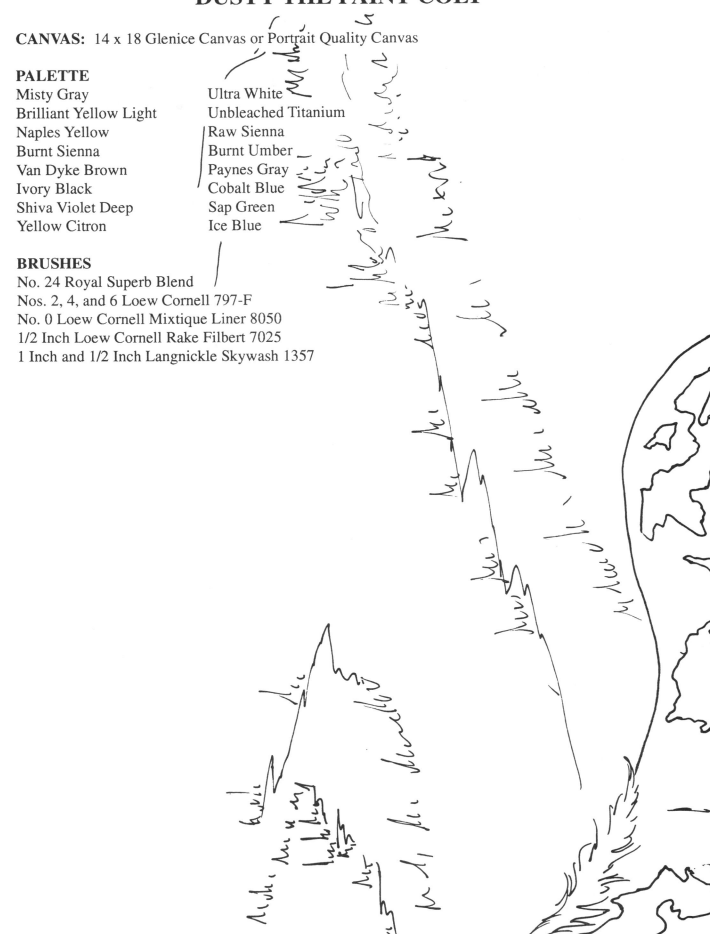

"DUSTY THE PAINT COLT"

WATERCOLOR BOOKS

Vol. 20	"Simply Country Watercolors" by Susan Scheewe Brown	257	$8.50	___
vol. 21	"Simply Watercolor" by Susan Scheewe Brown.....T.V. Book	260	$11.95	___
Vol. 22	"Watercolor For Everyone" by Susan Scheewe Brown.....T.V. Book	276	$11.95	___
Vol. 23	"Watercolor Step by Step" by Susan Scheewe Brown.....T.V. Book	294	$11.95	___
Vol. 24	"Introduction to Watercolor" by Susan Scheewe Brown.....T.V. Book	314	$11.95	___
Vol. 4	"Enjoy Watercolor" by Ellie Cook	210	$7.50	___
Vol. 6	"Watercolor Memories" by Ellie Cook	246	$8.50	___
Vol. 7	"My Favorite Things In Watercolor" by Ellie Cook	293	$8.50	___
Vol. 3	"Watercolor Made Easy 3" by Kathy George	301	$8.50	___
Vol. 1	"The Way I Started" by Gary Hawk	120	$6.00	___
Vol. 2	"Anyone Can Watercolor" by Ken Johnson	118	$6.50	___
Vol. 1	"Watercolor Fun & Easy" by Beverly Kaiser	243	$7.50	___
Vol. 1	"Flowers, Ribbon and Lace in Watercolor" by Linda McCulloch	280	$8.50	___

PEN & INK BOOKS / COLORED PENCIL BOOKS

Vol. 3	"Wings and Wildflowers" by Claudia Nice	135	$6.50	___
Vol. 6	"Journey of Memories" by Claudia Nice	166	$6.50	___
Vol. 7	"Scenes from Seasons Past" by Claudia Nice	183	$8.50	___
Vol. 8	"Taste of Summer" by Claidia Nice	223	$8.50	___
Vol. 9	"Familiar Faces" by Claudia Nice	284	$8.50	___
Vol. 2	"Colored Pencil Made Easy" by Jane Wunder	242	$7.50	___
Vol. 3	"The Beauty of Colored Pencil and Ink Drawing" by Jane Wunder	259	$7.50	___

VIDEOS BY SUSAN SCHEEWE BROWN

"The Gift Of Painting Simply Watercolor" 60 Minutes	$24.95	___
"The Gift Of Painting" 90 Minutes	$24.95	___
"Paintings For The Holidays" 60 Minutes	$24.95	___
"Watercolor & Oil Do Mix" 60 Minutes	$24.95	___
"Watercolor Special Effects" 60 Minutes	$24.95	___
"Fabric Painting Fun" 60 Minutes	$24.95	___

****
SHIPPING & HANDLING CHARGES

Add $2.50 for the First Book for shipping and handling.

Add $1.50 per each additional book.

Please Add $3.00 for handling & postage. PER TAPES. Sorry we must have a "NO REFUND - NO RETURN" policy.

U.S CURRENCY

PRICES SUBJECT TO CHANGE WITHOUT NOTICE.

WE ACCEPT
VISA
&
MASTERCARD

———— OILS BOOKS ————

Vol. 1	"His and Hers" by Susan Scheewe	101	$6.50	___	Vol. 3	"Winter Song" by Gloria Gaffney	271	$8.50
Vol. 6	"Brushed With Elegance" by Susan Schewe	106	$5.50	___	Vol. 1	"Roses Are For Everyone" by Bill Huffaker	145	$7.50
Vol. 7	"Paint 'n Patch" by Susan Scheewe	107	$5.50	___	Vol. 3	"Nature's Beauty" by Bill Huffaker	177	$6.50
Vol. 11	"I Love To Paint" by Susan Scheewe	111	$6.50	___	Vol. 1	"Copper, Silver, Brass & Glass" by susan Jenkins	211	$6.50
Vol. 14	"Enjoy Painting Animals" by Susan Scheewe	114	$6.50	___	Vol. 1	"In Full Bloom" by Susan Jenkins	313	$8.50
Vol. 17	"Countryside Reflections" by Susan Scheewe	161	$6.50	___	Vol. 1	"Backroads of My Memory" by Geri Kisner	225	$7.50
Vol. 19	"Gift Of Painting" by Susan Scheewe O/AC/WC	230	$8.50	___	Vol. 2	"Backroads of My Memory" by Geri Kisner	245	$7.50
Vol. 1	"Western Images" by Becky Anthony	186	$6.50	___	Vol. 2	"Country's Edge" by Shirley Koenig.....O/AC	212	$6.50
vol. 3	"Fantasy Flowers II" by Georgia Bartlett	129	$6.50	___	vol. 3	"Country's Edge" by Shirley Koenig.....O/AC	291	$8.50
vol. 4	"Soft Petals" by Georgia Bartlett	171	$6.50	___	vol. 1	"Ducks and Geese" by Jean Lyles	172	$6.50
Vol. 6	"Painting Fantasy Flowers" by Georgia Bartlett	215	$7.50	___	Vol. 1	"Raining Cats & Dogs" by Todd Mallett	304	$8.50
Vol. 7	"Flowers" by Georgia Bartlett	290	$8.50	___	Vol. 1	"Pathway To Painting" by Lee McGowan	281	$8.50
Vol. 8	"Petals" by Georgia Bartlett	317	$8.50	___	Vol. 1	"Stepping Stones" by Judy Nutter	121	$6.50
Vol. 1	"Painting, A Barrel of Fun"	194	$6.50	___	Vol. 1	"Rustic Charms" by Sharon Rachal	175	$6.50
Vol. 2	"Painting, a Barrel of Fun" by Donna Bell	201	$7.50	___	Vol. 2	"Rustic Charms II" by Sharon Rachal	199	$7.50
Vol. 3	"Barnscapes & More" by Donna Bell	218	$8.50	___	Vol. 3	"Rustic Charms III" by Sharon Rachal	217	$6.50
Vol. 4	"Countryscapes" by Donna Bell	249	$8.50	___	Vol. 4	"Rustic Charms IV" by Sharon Rachal	238	$7.50
Vol. 5	"Painter to Painter" by Donna Bell	263	$8.50	___	Vol. 5	"Rustic Charms V, Florals" by Sharon Rachal	261	$8.50
Vol. 6	"Landscapes With Acrylics & Oil" by Donna Bell	282	$8.50	___	Vol. 1	"Painting Flowers With Augie" by Augie Reis	152	$6.50
Vol. 1	"Natures Palette" by Carol Binford.....O/AC	248	$8.50	___	Vol. 2	"Painting Realism" by Judy Sleight	272	$8.50
Vol. 1	"Oil Painting The Easy Way" by Bill Blackman	219	$8.50	___	Vol. 1	"Soft & Misty Paintings" by Kathy Snider	204	$8.50
Vol. 1	"Mini Mini More" by Terri and Nancy Brown	150	$6.50	___	Vol. 2	"Soft & Misty Paintings" by Kathy Snider	229	$8.50
Vol. 2	"Mini Mini More" by Terri and Nancy Brown	151	$6.50	___	Vol. 2	"More Old Friends" by Gene Waggoner	148	$6.50
Vol. 4	"Heritage Trails" by Terri and Nancy Brown	169	$6.50	___	Vol. 4	"Friends We've Known" by Gene Waggoner	187	$7.50
Vol. 6	"Garden Trails" by Terri and Nancy Brown	283	$8.50	___	Vol. 5	"Friends Are Forever" by Gene Waggoner	231	$7.50
Vol. 2	"Windows of My World" by Jackie Claflin	181	$7.50	___	Vol. 1	"Fantasy Folk" by Don Weed	123	$6.50
Vol. 3	"Windows of My World 3" by Jackie Claflin	303	$8.50	___	Vol. 2	"Painting The Clowns" by Don Weed	124	$6.50
Vol.1	"Expressions In Oil" by Delores Egger	154	$6.50	___	Vol. 1	"Something Special For Everyone" by Mildred Yeiser	158	$6.50
Vol. 4	"Expressions In Oil" by Delores Egger	239	$7.50	___	Vol. 2	"Something Special For Everyone" by Mildred Yeiser	178	$6.50
Vol. 1	"Victorian Days" by Gloria Gaffney	240	$8.50	___	Vol. 5	"Soft & Gentle Paintings" by Mildred Yeiser	268	$8.50
Vol. 2	"Days of Heaven" by Gloria Gaffney	252	$8.50	___				

Susan Scheewe Publications Inc.

13435 N.E. Whitaker Way Portland, Or. 97230 PH (503)254-9100 FAX (503)252-9508